KATHERINE THOMSON began her career in the theatre as an actor. Her writing credits for the theatre include *Harbour*, *Kayak*, *Navigating*, *Diving for Pearls*, *Barmaids*, *A Sporting Chance*, *Darlinghurst Nights*, *This Hospital is My Country*, *Mavis Goes to Timor* and *Wonderlands*, all of which have been performed by Australia's leading theatre companies. Katherine has been writer-in-residence in Hong Kong (*Fragments of Hong Kong*), Kuala Lumpur and Eden, NSW (*Tonight We Anchor In Twofold Bay*). Television writing credits include *Blackjack*, *Grass Roots*, *Wildside*, *Fallen Angels*, *Halifax fp*, *GP* and *Something in the Air*. She has received five nominations for the New South Wales Premier's Literary Awards, and three nominations for Australian Film Institute Awards. Katherine has won three AWGIEs, and also the Louis Esson Prize for Drama in the Victorian Premier's Literary Awards. She is a director of the Sydney Theatre Company and is a Vice-President of the Australian Writers' Guild. Katherine is the recipient of the 2003 Rodney Seaborn Playwright's Award.

Scott Johnson as Tom and Pauline Whyman as Edie in the 2003 HotHouse Theatre production. (Photo: Jules Boag)

WONDERLANDS

KATHERINE THOMSON

Currency Press, Sydney

CURRENCY PLAYS

Wonderlands first published in 2004
by Currency Press Pty Ltd,
PO Box 2287, Strawberry Hills, NSW, 2012, Australia
enquiries@currency.com.au
www.currency.com.au
Reprinted 2014

In accordance with the requirement of the Australian Media, Entertainment & Arts Alliance,
Currency Press has made every effort to identify, and gain permission of, the artists who
appear in the photographs which illustrate this play.
NATIONAL LIBRARY OF AUSTRALIA CIP DATA
Thomson, Katherine, 1955–.
Wonderlands.
ISBN 0 86819 728 9.
1. Native title (Australia) – Drama. Country life – Drama. I. Title.
A822.3

Set by Dean Nottle
Cover design by Kate Florance
Front cover shows Pauline Whyman as Edie; back cover shows Scott Johnson as Tom and
Roger Oakley as Lon; both from the 2003 HotHouse Theatre production. (Photos: Jules Boag)
Currency Press acknowledges the Traditional Owners of the Country on which we live and
work. We pay our respects to all Aboriginal and Torres Strait Islander Elders, past and
present.

Foreword

Bob Munn

Drama is a matter of perception. It is often said that moments in time are packed or filled with drama. Events are said to be dramatic, lives are given to drama, people study drama...

Katherine Thomson has done what few people could achieve with the subject matter she chose for the play *Wonderlands*.

At the time of writing, the concept of Native Title for modern entertainment might be considered a taboo subject. To consider writing a play about it was almost incomprehensible. How would it be possible to fit such a damning, divisive and socially damaging subject into something that people could understand, let alone like?

Aboriginal people have been portrayed as a number of things in modern Australia—successful dancers, sportspeople, artists, an occasional star of television, but never as a cultural icon with specific rights under law to challenge the landholding class in Australian society.

The wonderful ability to travel forwards and backwards in time highlights the social and intellectual interaction between both tolerant and intolerant non-aboriginal people with the first Australians and the developing notion of what was bitter debate in the early stages of Native Title in much of rural Queensland. It shows how even complex issues can be simplified and how even the most simple things can be blurred by an unwillingness to understand other views.

Each moment in the time span of this play has been significant to me. It demonstrates the changing attitudes on a broad scale, but highlights the convenience of racism as an argument instead of proper discussion. If Aboriginal people who are part of the Native Title process wish to, they also might identify with the play. The same could be said of the Landholders.

The message remains the same all the way through this play. It does not manage to disguise empathy with the plight of Aboriginal people who have misplaced culture and language for a variety of reasons and social circumstances. The play does not treat anyone unfairly and is not a parody.

Katherine Thomson has an understanding of the motivation behind the need to lodge a native title claim. She accurately reflects the resistance to change, the folly of some actions and the huge need for mutual understanding.

If more people followed this lead, the reconciliation process may well be outdated.

Bob Munn
Gunggari Native Title claimant

Contents

Dedicated to Ethel Munn in appreciation of her wisdom, dignity, passion and patience.

Introduction

Henry Reynolds

This is a very good play. It is also a political play. Some readers may find these two statements contradictory despite the fact that some of the most successful plays at the moment in the West End and on Broadway are about political issues and the moral dilemmas faced by men and women as they confront the challenges of public life.

One of the elements that make *Wonderlands* such a fine political play is that it is not didactic: it doesn't preach and it isn't predictable. The characters are capable of carrying the themes of the play. They are autonomous and believable individuals with a past that we can readily imagine, well grounded in time and place. Thomson knows both well so she is able to set her play in rural Queensland and to unfold the drama created by unexpected events which had occurred in far away Canberra and, in particular, the decision of the High Court in the Wik Case in 1996.

It might not seem an ideal subject for an engaging play but a moment's thought will allow us to appreciate why Thomson set her play where she did. The Court, it might be remembered, decided that Pastoral Leases did not normally extinguish Aboriginal Native Title. This was a decision of almost revolutionary implications. Pastoral Leases covered vast areas of Outback Australia. They were the normal form of tenure for most pastoral families and had been so for two or three generations. Pastoralists thought of the land as theirs. Their families had often pioneered the land in question; had battled drought and flood and the banks; had buried grandparents and children and victims of accident. What is more, they often identified with their land.

Before the Wik decision, no one had challenged the tenure of leaseholders. They thought of themselves as proprietors with all the attendant status both in the country and in the Big Smoke. They were people of consequence. So Wik came like a thunderclap. Even when the case was underway all the advice given to Pastoralists was that a lease by definition provided all the rights of a freehold title. Queensland leaseholders felt even more secure because their leases, unlike those in the other states, contained nothing about Aboriginal rights of access and use.

The Wik decision, however, established that the Pastoral Lease was an inferior form of land tenure—little more than a license to use the land for pastoral purposes. That alone was a great blow to status and prestige. What was even worse was the possibility that Aborigines with traditional association with the land in question could now claim traditional rights to use the land for traditional hunting and gathering and for ceremonial purposes.

Clearly this outraged many pastoral families. Either many of the local Aboriginal families had been taken away to reserves and missions like Palm Island or Woorabinda or they lived on the outskirts of town in fringe camps and were at the very bottom of the hierarchy of status and esteem. What is more, the Pastoralists of the 1990s had forgotten the brutal conflict that had so often accompanied the establishment of the pastoral industry and the critical role of Aboriginal labour once that conflict came to an end. The Aborigines had forgotten neither.

For a few years after Wik there was a situation of tragic intensity. It passed largely unnoticed in urban Australia… at least in its specific, human detail. On the whole, people identified with either one side or the other. They were partisans lacking in empathy… or understanding. And this points to Katherine Thomson's great achievement. She humanises an otherwise abstract struggle over land and human rights and has turned it into compelling drama. We are all therefore in her debt.

Henry Reynolds is ARC Senior Research Fellow,
School of History and Classics, University of Tasmania.

Writer's Note

Katherine Thomson

Warm thanks to the actors who contributed so generously to the development of this play through the readings of previous drafts and the early workshop at HotHouse, and to the actors of the premiere production for their daring, enthusiasm, warmth, skills and inspiration. Much appreciation to HotHouse Theatre their commitment to this project and to Wesley Enoch and Marion Potts for their direction and dramaturgy.

While I spent time in Queensland researching the play—and thanks to those people who gave of their time, welcomed me into their homes, and walked with me explaining their country—this is a work of fiction. It is not based on any specific native title claim or outcome, or on any specific Aboriginal or non-Aboriginal community or individuals.

The (written) historical research for this play was particularly useful, particularly from Queensland where many were critical of the violent frontier wars that were being conducted in the late nineteenth century.

I was surprised to read of squatters such as Gideon Scott Lang, who had himself used the Native Police against Aboriginal people, speaking of eradication being accomplished with '… no more compunction or responsibility than if they [the Aborigines] were vermin… a cold blooded cruelty on the part of whites quite unparalleled in the history of these colonies'. [1]

In a series of articles in the *Queenslander* the editors wrote that settler behaviour 'fell far below British standards… we alone have descended to the 'kitchen lay' of extermination… a process which would shame us before our fellow countrymen in every part of the British Empire'.

The letters to the editors of Queensland papers by squatters and pioneers who were witness to massacres and murders pulled no punches either; writers expressing their shame at the barbarity and endeavouring to alert the nation to the extermination of Aboriginal inhabitants. These

---

[1] G.S. Lang, *The Aborigines of Australia, In Their Original Condition and in Their Relations with the White Man*, Melbourne: Wilson and McKennon, 1865.

letters were filled with passionate pleas that 'something be done', one cannot read them without a profound sense of regret that the writers were unable to influence the course of history.

But it's in the journals of the very first British settlers, for instance Watkin Tench or David Collins, that one has tantalising glimpses of very different relationships between black and white in the early days of Port Jackson. Read into a fishing trip one afternoon off Watson's Bay on the 28th February, 1791. A convict, William Bryant, is out fishing with Bennelong's sister, her two children and a little girl, and had the boat (filled with fish) not turned over, this was an excursion which probably would have gone unnoticed by the diarists of the day. Or picture David Collins in this colony, as he learns the Eora dialect, forms friendships with people like Barrangaroo and Darringha, is invited to ceremonies such as the famous initiation ceremony at Farm Cove in 1795. But this possibility of something 'other' was fleeting. It was soon lost in the Hawksbury Wars and the continuing landgrabs, fence-building and evictions from hunting ground and foreshore.

From Pamela Luke Watson's, *Frontier Lands and Pioneer Legends*,[2] I was led to the biographical works of Alice Duncan-Kemp whose family took up a lease in the Channel Country of Queensland in the late nineteenth century. As Watson points out in her comparison with other settlers of the same region, the Kemps were singular in that from their first arrival in the Channel Country the family was open to Aboriginal practice, tradition, knowledge, lore and law, and their lives were enriched accordingly. Needless to say these works were an inspiration for the character of Alice in this play.

As a non-Aboriginal Australian I have no choice but to understand our history in all its inspiration and shame. If we've missed out on 'being told', as we mostly have, then we're the losers if we don't make the effort to find out. Flexible minds will always triumph over hardened hearts.

Sydney
July 2004

---

[2] P.L. Watson, *Frontier Lands and Pioneer Legends, How Pastoralists Gained Karuwali Land*. Allen and Unwin, 1998.

First Production

Wonderlands was first produced by HotHouse Theatre at the Butter Factory Theatre, Albury Wodonga, on 13 June 2003, with the following cast:

CATHY	Annie Byron
JIM	Isaac Drandich
TOM	Scott Johnson
LON	Roger Oakley
ALICE	Gwyneth Price
EDIE	Pauline Whyman

Director, Marion Potts
Associate Director, Wesley Enoch
Designer, Ralph Myers
Lighting Designer, Rob Scott
Sound Designer, Max Lyandvert

Wonderlands was commissioned by HotHouse Theatre, Albury Wodonga. The creative development phase of *Wonderlands* was supported by the Myer Foundation.

CHARACTERS

EDIE, an Aboriginal woman in her 40s
CATHY, a white woman in her 40s
LON, a white man in his 40s or 50s
TOM, a white man in his 20s
ALICE, a white woman in her 30s
JIM, an Aboriginal man in his 20s

SETTING

Scenes take place on Ambertrue in 1931, a contemporary homestead, the riverbank, a paddock, a community hall, an office, and the street.

The original set was a packed red-earth floor, with a gumleaf-encrusted curtain snaking across the space, used to define acting areas as required. There was a single table for the household, and the rest of the acting space was bare.

The transitions between past and present were 'soft', scenes set in the present began while the 'past' characters were still on stage and vice versa.

At the end of the play the rear doors of the theatre opened, and Edie and Cathy walked out together into the night, towards the (actual) trees and the river beyond.

ACT ONE

Bush sounds. EDIE, CATHY, LON *and* TOM *appear.*

EDIE: Over the river. The other side of the river from here. On the second Yumba. Tin houses that grew like topsy, when's that hammering ever going to let up, our parents used to say. How many more extensions can that poor old excuse for a house take? Not always bodgy, sometimes good. Kerosene lights and long shadows across the circle of dirt grown smooth and bald from all those feet playing rounders for as late as you could as kids. Are you kids still playing rounders, school's tomorra. And casuarinas and trudging home from the pictures along the creek on a moonless night, the noise of old aunties playing cards to steer you home by. And good we're not on the run anymore. And Jim the water tank coming over selling water and weren't we mugs thinking that was all right when town water had been on for years. In town. Everyone knew everyone. Gambling away under the stars.

LON: When it's that still you can hear your own pulse. Some days that still you'd swear you can hear your old man. Watch that woody weed before it gets a hold. Clear as day. Everything's always sooner than you think.

TOM: Up the top of the second hill from the homestead. Not when the light bleaches everything to a blur, but morning time. Dusk. The top of the trees, you look down on them, they're making patterns like in paintings. If an artist came, they'd paint the trees, the horizon maybe, the red earth. One thing for certain is even if I was there with them they wouldn't paint me.

CATHY: When you open the gate to leave, there's a ridge that's been made in the soil. Over the years. The gate must have scratched and scraped that dirt and now there's an arc. And on top of that little arc, near the fence post, are a couple of flowers. Weeds really, that manage to grow. I notice them. And I'm always careful when I open the gate not to crush them. Tessie and Lon, sometimes they crush them,

but eventually they grow again. I don't say to them watch the weeds.
They're my secret, I suppose. My pact with the weeds. If a pact can
be one way.

Transition.

The heat of the day. LON *is waiting for* TOM, *who is repairing a fence,*
offstage.

LON: [*trying to find a rhyme*] Wedding… Wedding… Treading. Heading.
Bedding. Jesus. Heading…

> *Pause.*

>> Only yesterday it seems
>> That Tessie was on her first pony,
>> Today she's resplendent in white
>> And hitched to Tom Maloney.
>> As kids they played and raced their horses—

> TOM *enters during the following.* LON *repeats some of the poem*
> *for him.*

How's this? Dum de dum de dum, etcetera, bit of work needed at the
top then…

>> Today she's resplendent in white
>> And hitched to Tom Maloney.
>> As kids they rode and raced their horses
>> From Sanders End to Devil's Courses—

TOM: That's good.

LON: My darling Tessie has become Tom's bride,
>> Now they're up for a whole new ride.

> *Pause.*

I'll work on the last two lines.

TOM: Good. It's good.

LON: For the reception. It'll change. You need to think about it for a
while and… I'll work it up.

TOM: Wouldn't be an occasion without one.

LON: It's an occasion all right.

TOM: It will be.

LON: You're working up a sweat all right. Sorry I can't help.

TOM: Smoke-oh, eh. [*Pause.*] She's feeling the pressure, I think. Tessie. The wedding.

LON: Women get nervous.

TOM: Once she gets the dress right.

LON: Once she gets the dress right. That's right. [*He kicks his heel into the soil.*] You think how many times you've fallen on this. Hard as iron. Christ, I've had some falls on this.

TOM: If it's got four legs it can knock you down.

LON: You think back to those stock camps. Sleeping on the bare ground. I probably wouldn't get back up again these days.

TOM: You're going all right.

LON: Still, it can feel like a mattress when you've done a hard day's work. Until about three o'clock in the morning when the Bundy wears off.

TOM: True.

LON: Very few nights I haven't slept here, Tom, on this property. Very few nights in my life. On the few occasions I wasn't sleeping here I dreamt all night I was.

TOM: I had a dream the other night. About that fan belt in the generator.

LON: Dream how to fix the blasted thing?

TOM: Almost. Every night I shut my eyes and go come on, have that dream again, but this time don't wake up.

LON: We'll figure it out.

TOM: Yep.

LON: You know, when my father arrived out here to take over he was a city boy, all he knew about the land was that vegetables grew in it. No natural affinity whatsoever. Sure, he'd spent his Christmas holidays up here, to see the old aunty, and the spinster cousin Alice. I remember him saying after this cousin Alice died, and the will was read, and he came up here to take over, he scanned the property and felt like he'd been handed an orphan. This land was orphaned, and the stock was orphaned. But he knew he'd been called to set it right. And he lived up to the task that had been set. You get me? You get what I'm saying?

TOM: No.

LON: I'm not a well man.

> TOM *nods.*

I mean really not well.

TOM: You'll be right once you ease up a bit.

LON: You know what the specialist told me, Tom?

TOM: To go easy. Which is why I'm… go on.

LON: More than that. Thank Christ Cathy wasn't with me that day, she's high strung enough as it is just lately. This doctor, he looked me in the eye, and said I shouldn't be surprised if one day I just dropped down dead. I'd have thought being surprised about it'd be the least of my worries, but they were his words and I gleaned his meaning. After something like that you look at things differently.

TOM: I imagine you do.

LON: I do imagine. You look at things differently. What you might have done. You've done this. You've done that. You've kept this land going. You've developed runs, sunk bores, scraped through more droughts than you've had hot sausages, but you always think you could have done more.

TOM: You're getting better prices than some round here.

LON: What I'm trying to say is that for me to know that something's taken care of… that you're marrying Tessie, you'll take over, that if I cark it suddenly I won't be leaving this place orphaned. Or her orphaned for that matter. [*Pause.*] When Tessie said yes to you was one of the happiest days of my life. You know what you're doing. You've got your head screwed on.

TOM: Well, I was pretty chuffed. With Tessie you're never certain.

LON: You work like I did at your age. You know this country. You can anticipate what it'll throw at you, only way you can approach it. And your brother's still sweet about coming back to run your place…

TOM: Never wanted to leave in the first place.

LON: Long as that's still the plan.

TOM: Yep. Yep.

LON: She can fret about things, Tessie. It's only imagination, but get it started and she can't stop.

TOM: Her new colt days. That's what I call them.

LON: Yeah. That's it. Then it passes.

TOM: All things pass.

LON: She's more like one of those butterflies brushes past you and leaves a dusting. You wonder if it's got enough left on its wings to still be able to fly. Or for whatever they need that dusting for.

   Pause.

TOM: I'll take care of her. If she'll let me. [*Pause.*] I don't always understand how she wants me to be. What she wants.

LON: You can wither her or her mother in a look. Without a word.

TOM: I wouldn't. Wither her.

LON: If I do get a surprise, and drop dead… you will look after them both for me. I need to know if you'd do that.

TOM: Yes.

   Pause.

LON: The wedding can't come soon enough.

TOM: That's pretty much what I say.

   Pause.

LON: You'll be right shifting into the second homestead. You'll have privacy down there.

TOM: Right as rain.

LON: Cathy's running on adrenaline, of course.

TOM: She is. Ten years younger she's looking, I reckon.

LON: Yeah?

TOM: She just looks… more lively. Or something.

LON: Change of life.

TOM: Oh. Oh, right.

LON: Women thrive on weddings.

TOM: Right.

LON: I don't tell her everything. Cathy. She probably would be surprised. If I dropped dead. Unlike me, since I've been warned. Not to be surprised. Not sure how I'll manage that.

TOM: You'll outlive us all.

LON: Cathy of course, she thinks it's just angina.

TOM: Gotcha. Right. [*Pause.*] She promised to phone me. Tessie. When she got to town. It's been a week.

LON: Public phones.

TOM: True. [*Pause.*] But you've heard from her.

LON: Just once or twice. Quick calls. I think she did say she'd been trying to catch you.

TOM: Good. [*Pause.*] That's all I need to know. Give her a bit of… Well, this won't get a fence fixed.

LON: Once this medication kicks in, I'll be a bit more…

TOM: Take in the view. Go easy. Then we'll move up to Rowling's.

> *He goes.*

LON: You look for signs that you've achieved something. Not just something. Achieved your life.

1931.

ALICE *enters wearing a black dress.*

ALICE: Wait. Wait, Jim. Wait.

> JIM *enters, carrying a saddle bag. He's hot and sweaty, just ridden in from town.*

I've been looking for you since breakfast.

JIM: Just got back. Stayed another night at the Yumba.

ALICE: What are your plans for today?

> *Pause.*

JIM: Bits and pieces.

> *He starts to go.*

ALICE: Are you riding somewhere? Going out? [*Pause.*] Can I come with you then? [*Pause.*] If you're going to be riding.

JIM: I might just work round here.

ALICE: You're saddling up a new horse. You must be going somewhere. [*Pause.*] The minister left a paper from Sydney. They've joined the arches on the Harbour Bridge. I saved it for the boys—remember when we saw that newsreel?

JIM: I collected the post. Here. Plenty of it.

He gives it to her, then starts to go.

ALICE: Hold up.

JIM: I might want to check on the bores over west.

ALICE: Then I could come with you.

JIM: Might end up at Devil's Corner. Have to camp.

ALICE: I'll get my swag. And some extra tucker from Millie just in case.

JIM: You've still got your funeral mob here? Or they mostly gone or what?

ALICE: No. But drinking endless cups of tea and talking about Mother to relatives who hardly knew her isn't going to bring her back. I wish it would.

Pause.

JIM: I'll build you that memorial. A real good one. We'll get those stones and build it good.

ALICE: Today. We could go to the river today. Or another day. Another day. I don't care if you're riding to the tip and back, I'm coming with you. Just saddle Ginger while I get changed. We can talk through things while we ride.

JIM: What things is that?

ALICE: I'll tell you when we're out there.

She heads inside to change.

Present day.

The homestead. LON *is on the fixed phone,* CATHY *on the hands free. Their daughter is on the other end.*

CATHY: Tessie… Tessie…. I don't think she's still there. Are you still there, Tessie?

LON: It's your dad again, Tessie.

Pause.

CATHY: Speak to us, Tessie! Are you still there? [*Pause.*] Thank you.

LON: Good.

Pause.

CATHY: Your father's been saying how quiet it is. Without you. I've got leftovers every meal from lunchtime to breakfast. You'd think I could work out proportions after two weeks, but no. No. [*Pause.*] Does it seem to you like this dressmaker's taking a long time? Just wondering. It seems a long time to wait to be called back for the final fitting. Even for a wedding dress. What did Tom say, something funny. What was it, Lon, that Tom said? [*Pause.*] Something about getting a going-away dress as well, that maybe you're having a parachute stitched in so you can do a bunk. Something really funny like that. Ask us how we are. [*Pause.*] I'm terrific. Really well.

> *Pause.*

LON: As long as you're all right there at the Youth Hostel. [*Pause.*] You haven't lost your bus ticket or something. That happened to me once. Christ, I remember my father gave me a hiding.

CATHY: She's got a keycard. Unless you've lost that as well.

> *Pause.*

LON: Some brolgas flew in this morning. Beautiful they were. Wandering around near your orange tree. Beautiful. I was remembering the last time we had such a flock of brolgas, remember when that was.

> *Pause.*

CATHY: Yes, you do know, Tessie. It was the morning of your twenty-first, all those brolgas. You do know. [*Pause.*] Are you still there? Then talk to us, have a conversation. It's reverse charges remember. Tell us for instance about this dressmaker you've gone to. She hasn't sent us any kind of bill yet and we don't know her name. [*Pause.*] What's her name we were wondering? What street's she on? When does she think she'll finish your dress?

LON: It's all your choice, we don't mind it's someone new. We were just wondering her name.

CATHY: Say if you're standing outside the post office, is she left or right of there? On the main street? Whereabouts in relation to Dalgety's, for instance?

> *Pause.*

LON: Never mind. Bring a little map and we'll look when you get home.

CATHY: And, you know, I'm not even sure what fabric you've chosen.

LON: White, Mum. White. White.

CATHY: The new GP's arrived. That's something. Your father likes him, don't you Lon?

LON: Terrific.

CATHY: Lovely fellow. Indian. Dr Rash… Rashma… Anyway, it's on the receipt. I think they get a subsidy for coming out here. I think so. It's not good for your father's heart worrying why you're taking so long.

LON: You know what he said, this dark chap. After he'd asked our names. 'And where do you belong?' Must be an expression. For 'What's your address?' Where do you belong.

CATHY: How about I come down and join you? We could have a girls' night out. Come back home on the bus together. I might even buy myself another frock, I'm going off that blue thing.

LON: Frozen?

CATHY: Frozen?

LON: You don't mean literally you're frozen… it's thirty-five in the shade.

CATHY: She's joking, Dad.

LON: Yes, we're turning to ice up here, too. I'm just snuggling up to your mother right now to ward off hypothermia—

CATHY: Don't. [*To the phone*] What's that noise you're making?

LON: She's making shivering sounds. [*To the phone*] Princess, listen. Has someone spiked your drink or something? Is that what—?

> *Tessie has hung up.*

CATHY: That happened last time. As soon as you called her Princess…

LON: That's what I've always called her.

CATHY: Someone suggested that calling her that…

LON: What?

CATHY: Diminishes her. Treats her like a child.

LON: Which someone's that?

CATHY: Sorry?

LON: Who's the someone who knows our business?

> *Pause.*

CATHY: Me. I meant me. A figure of speech, it's what I think. That's what I think.

LON: Tessie wasn't a hundred per cent before she left.

CATHY: That's true.

LON: But she's in love.

CATHY: Let's hope so.

LON: And nervous about the wedding.

CATHY: She could be having second thoughts. What if she does have second thoughts?

LON: Then she'll have third ones. She's marrying Tom.

CATHY: Maybe she doesn't love him as much as she thought. Perhaps it's all too tied up with Tom taking over here.

> *Pause.*

LON: She just needs to be stronger. Strong enough to run a homestead, be a wife. What?

CATHY: That's a tall order, Lon. Strong enough to be a wife.

1931.

JIM *enters, followed by* ALICE. *They've been riding, fast. Both are out of breath, hot.* JIM *carries a sack and a spade.*

ALICE: Well, that didn't work, did it? [*Pause.*] You were hoping we'd turn back. You were. 'Fess up.

JIM: Not me, Miss Alice.

ALICE: Or trying to lose us. One or the other.

JIM: Stardust needed a run, that's all.

ALICE: A run? That wasn't a run, that was a heat for the Melbourne Cup. God.

> *Pause.* JIM *kneels down, scraping off some rocks and soft clay, surreptitiously testing the quality.*

JIM: You know the ring-barkers are just about finished over at the Stevens place. [*Pause.*] You might want them here.

ALICE: I'm not sure.

JIM: They'll be finished there by the end of the week.

ALICE: What do you think?

JIM: Not up to me, up to you.

Pause.

ALICE: You might as well tell me what I've done. You're shirty as all get-out. You might as well tell me what I've done. Or haven't done.

Pause.

JIM: You're in charge of Ambertrue now. You're the one's got to make decisions. Start planning. You're the boss.

ALICE: So we should get the ring-barkers here. To do that section of the eastern run.

JIM continues looking at the rocks, finding one that he wants. He prises it up and into a sack.

What are you doing with those?

He doesn't answer.

The silence was deafening. Alice was puzzled. What transgression had she made, what on earth had she done?

JIM: [*not listening*] Sorry?

ALICE: Two can play at this game, Jim. The day's yours. You won. You want to be on your own, well so do I. [*She starts to head back to the horses.*] We'll discuss the next few months when you're in a better mood.

JIM: What do you mean?

ALICE: What I said. You're barely civil.

JIM: About the next few months.

ALICE: We'll sit down with the calendar. Decisions have to be made, you're right.

JIM: What decisions exactly?

ALICE: The whole flaming lot, Jim. The new hayshed for starters. Before the old one falls down.

JIM: So you'll build the hayshed?

ALICE: And I need your advice. Oh, don't look so surprised, Jim. There hasn't been so much as a shed or a doghouse on this land without you or your father telling Mother and me where it should go. Why should anything change? The homestead's where it is because your grandfather marked it out on the dirt.

JIM: Are you saying you won't be going back then? With the funeral mob.

ALICE: That's never even entered my head. Is that what you thought, that I'd walk off here? What sort of bulldust's that? Back to where? This is my home.

JIM: When you said you wanted to talk about things…

ALICE: A book I'm writing…

JIM: A book?

ALICE: A book. A history of Ambertrue. From the day Papa came until now. I started it when Mother became ill. About everyone who's ever worked here, lived here. How your parents taught me the country when I was a child. And the tribes we used to come across. But there are things I've forgotten and Yirralong words I can't remember and I thought wouldn't it be a good thing to do, to ride out with Jim and start seeing whether we can't fill in some of the gaps.

JIM: Right.

ALICE: But how dare you think I'd walk off Ambertrue. How dare you, Jim.

JIM: Keep your hat on.

ALICE: How dare you think I'd give this up. It really takes the cake. Is that why the other blacks have all been acting strange? I give you my word I'm staying. Take it or leave it, up to you.

> JIM *hesitates, then walks some distance away in search of another piece of clay.*

Present day.

Bush sounds. EDIE *is speaking to the old people, in her mind.*

EDIE: People are reasonable. And you don't know, Grannie, they've probably been expecting it, some sort of Native Title claim, somewhere down the line. They must have been. The letters are out, they've gone. From the Yirralong people. Possess, occupy and enjoy is how you have to put it, blanket-like. To exercise our Native Title Rights, rights meaning that we've always had them. And people are reasonable, once we talk through what it all means… In practical terms it's sweet bugger-all we'll get, but it's the spirit of the thing over legal carry-on, and the pastoralists'll realise that. Give the kids back some knowledge before it's too late. According to the lawyers the most we can hope for is to have a say if they want to build something over a site, and to be able to take the kids onto leases for a camp. But it'll be in writing. Recognised as Yirralong country, it'll say so in whitefella law. This is the country your ancestors looked after. Your great great great great great great great... Remember we used to play that game in the back of the car see how far you could go back 'til Dad'd say stick a sock in it. And now it's yours to watch over, we'll be saying to the young ones. Now you look after it too when you visit there. They're not a bad lot, the whites round here, they'd've been expecting this, for sure. Even my Steve's taken an interest the last few days, lawyers on and off the phone and picking me up at the airport. So if nothing else comes of this but Steve gets interested in more than that wretched *nyadi*, that's a victory in itself. But, by God, we had to claim over a helluva lot. Up past Sommervilles' lease, past Terribong, down Derry Downs, and a bit of a curve to Stanfords'. And some scraps of Crown Land and old Telstra land. You can get nervous if you think about it too much. That the connection report could be better, we could've done with a few of you folk hanging on for a few more years for that, given us a bit more detail. Along with a few more anthropologists sticking their noses in. Still, as Lorraine said, weren't we lucky some of our old Aunties loved a gossip? We'd never have found out half we needed except for them. Their side'll try to shoot holes all through it, the connection report, and we'll have to argue why we haven't had continuous connection... but name me a mob who has round this part of the state. The lawyer wouldn't have let us proceed if he didn't think we had a chance. I keep saying to him, all this work and you don't take a penny, reckons he wants to do his bit. And he's in for the long haul, he said that. Then there'll be this latest bullshit that we Yirralongs were blow-ins from down south, don't go crook, I heard Colin Whelan going on about that at the bowling club. God, he's a terrible piece of work. They *are* a cloud on the horizon, Colin Whelan's mob. Whoever half of them are. First half of them ever heard they were Karunya was when the ATSIC grant went in. He's been sucking up to ATSIC something shocking, they must have got wind of our claim. Colin knows as well as we do they came from down south a hundred-odd years back if they're lucky. Camped on old man Whelan's place and took his name, but if Colin's convinced himself otherwise… Well, we can't worry about that. People are reasonable. Even Colin Bloody Whelan.

1931.

ALICE *and* JIM *enter.* ALICE *claps some stones together, trying to jog* JIM*'s memory.*

ALICE: That's the sound they made. Don't you remember that tribe?

JIM: Most of the real old blackfellas were gone by the time I was born. You know more about my mob than I do half the time.

ALICE: I would have been about ten, so I suppose it was before you were born. Your mother and father, and me. Out looking for survey pegs. And we camped and it was pitch dark and across the gully we heard this sound. Over some chanting. The sound of stones. [*She claps them to a crescendo.*] Chattering—stone chatter, that's what your father called it. Talking to each other through the night. It was a feature of this particular tribe. Did he ever talk about them? They'd visit once a year.

JIM: That's right…

ALICE: But did he ever say their name, your father? [*Pause.*] He wouldn't let us come with him visiting their camp. It was a tribe renowned for being gossips. But he'd never tell me the gossip. What's the gossip, I asked him when he came back to us, and he roared laughing. And wouldn't tell. They'd travel across the country trading. And star legends. That was the other thing they were known for. Maybe I could come with you next time you go to the Yumba. See if Uncle Arthur knows. Or one of the others. If you write a book you have to get things right.

JIM: They won't.

ALICE: They might.

JIM: They won't.

ALICE: Or I could give you a list of Yirralong names I need for things. And you could ask them. They wouldn't mind if you told them what it was for. Get them interested.

JIM: Long story, Miss Alice. But they've had enough of lists.

He stands and picks up the hessian sack.

ALICE: What's it for, Jim? This clay.

JIM: Some questions, Miss Alice, you don't want to know.

JIM *heads off to the horses,* ALICE *follows.*

Present day.

LON *is on the phone, popping a heart pill.*

LON: Sandra. Sandra. Of course I'm not saying you know where she is. You're her aunt, that's all and… I just thought on the off chance that she'd headed off to the bright lights of Brisbane on some sort of personal hens night, I don't know. I don't know what's going on inside her head. [*Pause.*] She went to Toowoomba for a fitting for her wedding dress and she's been gone a fortnight. [*Pause.*] Of course I've phoned the police, but there's not a lot they can do. Then yesterday we get this envelope in Tessie's writing. From Tessie. A blank postcard from the youth hostel where she was staying, along with a piece of black material. Dress material. Black. Cathy had asked her when she arrived to send us a sample of the fabric. Of this dress I'm meant to be paying for. That's what she sends. Black. [*Pause.*] It's got nothing to do with Tom, she loves Tom. Worships Tom. But she's not herself, not by a long shot. So if you get any funny calls from Tessie… [*Pause.*] Cathy's mother? Yes, she did. You're right. She did. Cathy's mother went very odd. And she wasn't all that old. That's true. Christ. [*Pause.*] What? What's that supposed to mean, punishment? You said we were being punished—what exactly do you mean? [*Pause.*] Here we go, here we go. You're as mad as a two-bob watch Sandra, never mind anyone else. You want to run this dried-up, windswept shit of a property you come up and do it. If it's worried you all these years, we'll leave the gate open, walk on in. Listen to me, and this is the last time I say this. When Dad died either you bought me out or I bought you out. Not a property around here where siblings didn't have to walk off. You agreed to my offer. It's why you're sitting in your little unit. And yes it is worth more now, but so are my teeth—to me—and if it's any consolation it'll be worth fuck-all if I drop dead in my tracks and/or if Tessie doesn't do the right thing and marry Tom who does know how to run cattle among his other assets. This is history, Sandra, history. Bit of advice. Lugging history on your back's a sure-fire way to become a pain in the neck. [*Pause.*] I hope to see you at the wedding, Sandra. I sincerely hope.

CATHY *enters with mail.*

1931.

JIM *calls across the space.*

JIM: Stay there! Don't move! Don't move!

Present day.

LON: [*at the phone*] You silly, bloody, twisted bitch. Sandra.
CATHY: Why did she phone?
LON: I thought Tessie…
CATHY: She doesn't like her. As if she'd go there.
LON: Dad'd fling himself around in his grave the things she comes out with. [*Pause.*] You know when all this business with Tessie started, and I'm right on this. The year she stopped going out mustering. She started going all… inward…
CATHY: You're the one who stopped her, Lon.
LON: A young girl camping out with a bunch of blokes, what's a man supposed to do?

    Pause.

CATHY: Perhaps she's just wanted to go away on her own. For a while. She is an adult after all.
LON: It's not some other bloke…
CATHY: Tessie?
LON: What age was your mother when she started going strange?
CATHY: Don't.
LON: Piece things together. That episode at Easter when she started babbling away, when we were driving along. Going on and on about the rocks or some damned thing. These weird calls. This postcard.

It's in the genes. Your mother that first Christmas I had with your family, out in the clothesline in her slips and suspenders while the turkey was burning to a crisp. Talking to the cockatoos.

CATHY: She went through a bad patch.

LON: And her brother, good old Uncle Ed—

CATHY: Ted.

LON: What'd he do? Try to walk bare-foot to Bourke and back? [*Pointing to his head*] Zing zing.

CATHY: Why don't you start on me, Lon? I suppose I'm mad too.

LON: Well, I'm watching you through the window just right now smiling away to yourself. In a world of your own. Daughter's missing, but you're smiling away.

CATHY: I'll go and look for her, how's that?

LON: We're pretty certain she's left Toowoomba. Or not. So that should narrow it down.

> *Pause.*

CATHY: There's a vehicle coming. Tom. It's Tom. I'll put the jug on.

1931.

JIM *runs across the space.*

JIM: [*calling*] The best thing to do is don't move... [*To the horse*] Jesus, Ginger—you idiot of a horse... don't move!

Present day.

TOM *enters. He hands some mail to* LON.

TOM: Brought your mail up.

LON: Cheers.

TOM: No card from Tessie. I checked. [*Pause.*] Heard from her yet?

LON: No.

CATHY: Yes.

LON: Yes.

CATHY: Yes, she rang to say every time I try to call Tom he's either not there or the phone's engaged. Or the public phone's not working.

That's the thing, I think. Those public phones. She seems to keep losing her phone card. But she's having a lovely time, choosing things for the wedding. She's going to look lovely from how she describes the dress.

TOM: She did call me.

CATHY: Oh, she did. Oh, good.

TOM: She said she was still in Toowoomba.

CATHY: Did she say she'd left the youth hostel? We're not quite sure where she's staying.

TOM: Then Shirley Thomas spoke to a mate of mine arrived here yesterday, Shirley Thomas saw her way down Barlow way that same day. Barlow's three hundred ks away.

LON: She could do that in a day.

TOM: That's really why I came by. To see what she might be doing down Barlow. If you knew why she'd say she was staying in Toowoomba and be in Barlow.

CATHY: She's got a second cousin there. On my side. She must be showing her the fabric. And things. The garter. All that.

LON: I'll be calling her then. Give her a piece of my mind. She should be on her way home.

TOM: My first thought was she's hitched up with another bloke.

LON: No.

CATHY: Not Tessie.

TOM: That that's why she's been acting strange.

LON: You got a bit to learn about women, Tom, they are strange, that's the whole point.

TOM: Shirley Thomas said she didn't look…

LON: What?

CATHY: What, Tom?

TOM: Quite right.

LON: [*turning to* CATHY] Did your second cousin in Barlow make mention of Tessie looking not quite right?

CATHY: No. No, she didn't say that. Not at all.

TOM: Shirley said they met up crossing over the bridge just before town. Tessie was just standing there. Watching faces float down the river, she said.

CATHY: Faces?

TOM: I know. And the river's been dry for years.

LON *distracts himself by opening the mail.*

LON: She was being poetic. She's very poetic, Tessie.

TOM: That's good to know she's with family. I was thinking, you know…

LON: Yes…

CATHY: Yes…

TOM: Could you give the cousin a ring while I'm here?

CATHY: Tessie's naughty, she really is. She says that sort of thing to sound interesting or something. They're harvesting through the day, we'll have to try them tonight. [*Pause.*] She said last time she called, tell Tom I love him very much.

TOM: Cheers.

CATHY: And… she sent a sample of wedding dress fabric, lovely white shot silk. She said when you've had a look pass it on to Tom. I wonder… I wonder where I put that small piece of white silk.

By now LON *has opened one of his letters. He reads it.*

1931.

JIM *is helping* ALICE *to her feet.*

LON: [*reading*] What the fuck…?

ALICE: Ow ow…!

LON: [*reading*] You have got to be bloody joking.

ALICE: Hold on… Aaaaah…!

LON: You have got to be bloody joking.

ALICE: Not like that!

LON: Not this. Not this. Jesus wept! No!

CATHY: What is it, Lon?

LON: You wouldn't flaming read about it—

CATHY: Why are you holding your chest? [*To* TOM] He's got a pain. Get some water.

LON: This is—this is—

CATHY: [*to* LON] Whatever this is, calm down. [*To* TOM] And his pills on the bench. [*To* LON] Is it Tessie? Just say, just nod.

LON: This is… Answer me this. Answer me this. Who the hell are the Yirralong people?

> TOM *enters with the water.* LON *doesn't take his pill.*

Who or what are the Yirralong people when they're at home?

TOM: Er… the cultural centre co-op place.

CATHY: They've got that office, take your pill.

LON: What office would that be? The TAB, the top pub—that office?

CATHY: Are they wanting money? They get money.

LON: [*to* TOM] You haven't got your mail yet, then.

TOM: You're always well ahead of me.

> LON *passes him the letter.*

CATHY: Tell me what it is, Tom. [*To* LON] Your blood pressure's rising just to look at you.

TOM: [*reading*] Possess, occupy and enjoy… according to their rights…

LON: We'll deal with this, it's not going to happen. Someone's put her up to this, I know Edie Jordan, this isn't her. She's signed the bloody thing. Someone's put her up to it. Some city quarter-caste or worse, that'd be. Look at the bowling club, for Christ's sake. Who's president? A darkie's president. Colin Whelan, for Christ's sake.

TOM: He's blonde Colin, I always forget—

LON: He wouldn't be in this. The only native rights Colin Whelan wants to assert is the right to improve his handicap.

CATHY: It's not as if we've been… You all played cricket with them as kids. They've always been on the cricket team.

LON: From day one. Paul Keating. This is all him, all him—

CATHY: The doctor said no stress.

LON: I mean it's not enough we've got Pie in the Sky checking if you've let one tree drop that shouldn't have…

TOM: They sit front row at the pictures only because of habit.

LON: We all went to the same school! That's why all this is a mistake. And here's the million-dollar question. Ever in your life, ever in your life, have you ever heard the word Yirralong in your life? Of course not.

> *Pause.*

TOM: There was the Yirralong lullaby. Old Sarah taught it to Dad. He taught it to me. In the lingo if I can remember it…

LON: Well, we won't be singing that to the lawyers.

CATHY: There'll be lawyers.

LON: It's a Native Title Claim, Cathy. Written by lawyers for lawyers. Edie Jordan being the patsy. It'll cost us money, no doubt about it.

Pause.

TOM: They weren't a match for us, of course. I often think about that. Spears. Versus guns.

LON: They weren't here.

TOM: They were here.

LON: There aren't any permanent water courses across this property, or yours. They weren't here. And they never had spears.

TOM: They'd dig those deep bush wells.

CATHY: Tea, Tom? And, Lon, take that pill.

TOM: I'm right. But when you think about it…

LON: What?

TOM: Remember that old station journal and your… who was it, that lady relation's old notebook? Lot of blacks mentioned in that, by name, all the old customs and that. According to Tessie.

CATHY: She did a project on those books once. When she was in sixth class. She got it out from somewhere. Remember how tiny the writing was…? And how it just turned to scribble at the end? Writing over and over on the one spot on the page?

LON: Get this out of your system. They were works of fiction. Some passing teacher, they were always drunks in those days, some passing alky teacher fancied himself a novelist and wrote as if he was from here. A novel. The beginnings of a work of fiction. That's all that was.

CATHY: Wonder what happened to them, though?

LON: It doesn't really matter because it wasn't anything.

CATHY: I thought—

LON: Thrown out. Gone. [*Pause.*] We'll be able to knock this on the head, but it'll have to be a united job.

TOM: Yep.

LON: Only person's getting my land is you, Tom.

TOM: I wouldn't put it like that. Like I'm doing a take-over job. It's Tessie and me.

CATHY: What do we do about this? You read about these things dragging on for years.

LON: Which is why we pay our dues. National Farmers'll be down on this like a ton of bricks. This is war. My family's been here one hundred and nineteen years, Tom. One hundred and nineteen years. You've seen the gravestones. We'll organise the biggest meeting this area's ever seen.

CATHY: The doctor said no stress.

LON: My grandchildren will live on this land!

TOM: I should go home and see if I've got one.

LON: You'll have one. [*After him*] Tell me what I just said.

TOM: Your grandchildren will live on this land.

LON: Too right.

1931.

JIM *is pouring water over a cloth, pressing it to* ALICE's *forehead.*

ALICE: That's enough... that's half your water. Head over turkey. Yow! She baulked at something.

JIM: She was playing up all last week. Always feels all right, that moment, flying through the air. Then you gotta come down.

ALICE: [*laughing*] Don't make me laugh... Ow...! At least I've got a thick skull.

JIM: Long as you're not seeing stars.

ALICE: Mary Pickford /

JIM: [*overlapping*] Douglas Fairbanks.

ALICE: Ow! Well, I'll have an impressive bump. But no broken bones.

JIM: We'll just wait a spell.

ALICE: Now I'm holding you up.

JIM *shrugs. He kicks over some rocks as he paces around. He notices something in the rubble.*

What've you found?

JIM: An old chopper... too right... that's what it is.

She holds out her hand. He gives it to her.

ALICE: It fits my hand.

JIM: Yours if you want it.

She hands it back to him.

ALICE: Put it back. We've never had a collection, I'm not about to start now.

Pause.

JIM: Sorry you fell.

ALICE: You didn't push me.

JIM: I was going too fast.

ALICE: You've got a bee in your bonnet about something.

JIM *nods.*

You and Dora?

JIM: No more than usual. No.

Gwyneth Price as Alice and Isaac Drandich as Jim in the 2003 HotHouse Theatre production. (Photo: Jules Boag)

ALICE: Is it because you don't believe me, that you think I won't last, and I'll leave. All I can give you is my word. Or because I'm writing this book? [*Pause.*] Think ahead to thirty, forty, fifty years time. Australia in the future, imagine what it might be like. People should know how differently we lived with the old blacks. How here on Ambertrue we didn't chase them off. Maybe there'll be a time when people won't believe that you could go out riding and hear that stone chatter or… The things your parents taught me, they're the sort of things that I'm putting down in the book. Like the time of the boy at the sandhill… Remember we used to talk about that?

JIM: No.

ALICE: Yes you do. That boy who just jumped out of a bush and started whacking me and my horse—I was ten, before you were born—and my mare was trying to throw me—sounds familiar—but this boy just kept hitting me with his coota—and your parents ride up going crook on *me* for trying to whip the stick out of his hand. He was a second degree initiate, his job was to guard the well. What was that expression of your father's…? Learn your brains from your elbow, Alice. Remember he used to say that?

Pause.

JIM: They're having a round-up. The coppers. Under the Act. Moving everyone out of town. And off Derry Downs, off Terribong.

ALICE: Who?

JIM: Just about everyone on the Yumba. Yirralong mob, Karunyah mob, doesn't matter who. About five hundred of 'em.

ALICE: To where?

JIM: They're saying that Palm Island. Or that other big place nearly to Brisbane.

ALICE: So far away…

JIM: Everyone's too sick to fight. Some of Millie's family bolted, the rest of 'em's too tired. So Uncle Arthur wants to take ochres with him from this country. He told me four different spots and that's where the ochre's gotta come from. Everyone's saying, Uncle, where we're going they don't let you dance, but he's saying, what sort of place don't let you dance? If we get to them all today I can take them into him tomorrow.

ALICE: We've seen this coming. All the big stations breaking up into smaller blocks. [*Pause.*] It might be for the best. They'll be fed, the children clothed, be able to see doctors...

JIM: Me, my boys, the stockyard boys and Dora, we'll be the last of the Yirralong in these parts.

ALICE: School, too. The children can go to a proper school.

JIM: Miss Alice. If ever you plan to give the nod, to send us off, we'd prefer to know. We'd prefer to go on the run, take our luck fencing, droving further south. I've thought about this, I've got a way planned to go.

ALICE: You've got a job here for as long as you like. Everyone with jobs here, if you have a job you're not under the Act.

JIM: All it takes is you to give the nod.

ALICE: I know. But it's not going to happen.

JIM: That's what they thought. [*Pause.*] You know what's been churning through my mind? That Yirralong lullaby. How I never want to hear that bloody song again.

Present day.

CATHY *is waving off* TOM.

CATHY: He was right about those books, Tom. It wasn't a novel. It was notes about the old blacks. And the original station journal from the very first days.

LON: Jesus wept! You're not a loose cannon, you're a cannon careering over the decks and down the stairs. Into the captain's quarters. That was half a novel or something, it was fiction. Fantasy. All made up. A couple of blacks might have shown old Major Mitchell which track led where, but they did not live here. You know nothing about those books because they didn't exist. We tread carefully, Cathy. This is like a war, loose lips and so on.

CATHY: What on earth are we going to do? Faces in the river. Dear sweet Tom. Anyone else'd run a mile.

LON: It can all be solved. Nothing that can't be solved. Next time she calls you, you find out where she is. Who she's staying with in Barlow. If she's still there.

CATHY: She won't say.

LON: Clues. You get clues. You pay attention to detail. Background noises. And we get the police and we bring her back home. There's no reason on earth she shouldn't marry that man. [*Pause.*] Get her straight to this new doctor. They can treat these things. Jeff Kennett. Your job's to get our daughter home. My job's to save the farm.

Transition.

EDIE, LON, TOM *and* CATHY *are at the meeting of the pastoralists and graziers.* LON *stands on a chair.*

LON: For those of you latecomers, the bloke from central office missed his plane, so I was asked to chair the meeting. And I might as well read this again—a fax this morning from the Prime Minister. [*Reading*] 'Rest assured you will not be put off your land. We will never allow that to happen.' That just about says it all. That this is a threat and that it's imperative that we act. Never mind what kind of lease you've got.

EDIE: [*sotto*] God help us.

TOM *raises his hand.*

LON: Tom Maloney.

TOM *stands, he has notes.*

TOM: I suppose what I want to say is you think the Native Title bizzo's what happens in Torres Strait or the Kimberleys or further west. But here we are in the same shit, excuse my language. And we all pay our fees to this get-up. So we want value for our fees. Because the other side's going to have teams of lawyers coming out of their ears like the Magic Pudding. Already the government's freezing leases while they fight other claims, we've got the banks not wanting to lend money on something that might disappear. I know the banks are bastards but all the more reason… [*Lost for words*] It's a worry.

TOM *sits.*

LON: If I can speak from the chair for a moment—the way I look at it is this. We've made this country work and we've made it ours. And it's not an easy country. It's country that takes from us and it takes from us and we keep saying yes and coming back for more because—and I don't want to get too flowery over this—but it *is* us. They're trying to ask us to chop off our arm. Drain our blood.

EDIE *raises her hand.*

EDIE: Excuse me, Mister Chair.

LON: [*surprised*] Edie Jordan…

EDIE: With respect to you and to our Prime Minister…

LON: Edie, just to save you any embarrassment, this is members only. For people to have their say.

EDIE: I run cattle, Lon. I've been a paid-up member for years.

A pause as EDIE *fields a comment from someone in the meeting.*

On freehold land that I own. That I paid for. [*Pause.*] Not with a grant, a loan. [*Pause.*] Maybe I am the nigger in the woodpile, whoever said that so descriptively, but God knows the woodpile's where most of the men who worked your properties had to eat their tucker in the old days, so maybe I'm in good company.

Scott Rankin as Tom in the 2003 HotHouse Theatre production. (Photo: Jules Boag)

LON: If I can ask you to get to your point.

EDIE: No one can take your land away. You know that as well as I do. But your newspapers, this organisation that claims to be a peak body, National Party members who should know better, they're taking you all for fools. Whipping up a storm.

LON: 'To consult with leaseholders' activities such as laying fences, roads, boards or any land-moving activity.' They're the words you've signed off on. They're more than a storm, they're a full-on tempest. They're a declared national disaster.

EDIE: And if you think through what that means—

LON: It covers just about anything we do—

EDIE: If such an activity affected any nominated sites—look, I didn't come here for a slanging match—any sites designated in the connection report. [*Pause.*] The connection report's available in our office. Our office is two hundred and fifty metres up the road.

LON: With respect, Edie, I think I'm speaking for the entire meeting when I say that the only full-caste Aboriginal ever walked my place was either on their way to somewhere else or lost.

EDIE: Can we please raise the level of this debate—?

LON: Guaranteed there wasn't.

EDIE: Walking off because your father hadn't paid them their wages more like it.

LON: My father paid every single half-caste, quarter-caste and quadroon—

EDIE: And you've walked the length and breadth of your property, have you? You've never seen a stone scatter? Never looked under a rocky outcrop, seen a faded painting?

LON: Have I ever seen a painting? That's a good question. Yeah, I have, Edie. One. The only painting I've seen done by blacks in a hundred-mile radius was the shelter shed at the stockyards, done for sit-down money, and if I recall it's still never got past the undercoat.

TOM: Apparently the urn's ready, for morning tea.

EDIE: I really came here to say, that if anyone's got any questions about the claim, about the legislation—our office is two hundred and fifty metres up the road.

TOM: They've set it up on the verandah.

EDIE: Surely the more we share our history, it's not just ours, it's yours… If any of you had any brains you'd realise—

She stops herself.

LON: Go on, Mrs Jordan. If we had any brains. If we had any brains we'd be asking why one tiny percentage of the Australian population wants privileges over another.

EDIE: They're rights. It's exercising rights. Under the law. Looking to the future, I don't see we have any choice.

LON: Here's mine. Here's my choice. And we'll get to morning tea. Do I honour my father and carry on his hard, hard work, or am I known forever as the one who threw up his hands—?

EDIE: No one's asking you to—

LON: Threw up his hands and handed it all over to a mob of half-castes who think that bashing two sticks together entitles them to what is mine? Do I want to have my wife tripping over strangers on their way to wander at will, shoot at my prime cattle? That won't happen on my watch.

EDIE: It won't happen anyway—

LON: Not on my watch, it won't. And you know why it won't? Because you'll lose. You lost the first day people came up here. It was survival of the fittest and you lost. And we survived here. And it kills you. Your families are wrecks and your men bash you senseless and your livers are shot with the drink and your churn out the same old rubbish that the land talks to you or something. Well, you know what we all feel like saying if only we had the guts? Change the record, it's boring us all to tears. But you won't because if you keep saying it loud enough you know there'll be a handout in it. But you know the irony? You'd be better off letting all that go. It's chains around your feet. Holding you all back to a time that didn't exist anyway. It was survival of the fittest, you lost and you're very poor losers. Very poor losers indeed. [*Pause.*] Now, let's look to the future. Morning tea.

1931.

ALICE *is still shaky from the fall. She looks up.*

ALICE: What on earth is that? Look.

JIM *follows her gaze upwards.*

JIM: What the hell…? A rock…

ALICE: A meteor, but it's too slow.

JIM: What's falling off it…?

ALICE: Feathers, feathers, it's a bird…

JIM: No, it's not… it's two birds…

ALICE: Two birds. Digging into each other—you can see the talons, look. They're fighting. In mid-air…

JIM: They'll be hitting the ground together at this rate—

The 'birds' spring apart. ALICE *and* JIM *watch them fly off in different directions.*

ALICE: A buzzard.

JIM: And an eagle.

ALICE: They did all that without a sound.

JIM: Fighting over a nest.

ALICE: They've gone. Who won?

JIM: No one.

Pause.

ALICE: People could come and camp here. Uncle Arthur, he'll die if he has to go away.

JIM: He'd be wanting to take care of the others. Get them there. Watch over them. Sooner or later Welfare'd come. But you know what gets up my goat? Why they aren't putting up a fight. Yirralong used to be warriors. Blood should be flowing in the river, fight to the death before we get taken away.

ALICE: I don't know what to say.

Pause.

JIM: You rest here, next place I'm going you can't go. Save yourself for the ride across to Good Luck Camp. I'll be about an hour.

ALICE: I'll write down the story of the buzzard and the eagle.

JIM: There's something else. Something in my saddlebag I've got to give you.

ALICE: A headache powder, my prayers are answered!

JIM: Something I collected in town.

> *He leaves.*

Present.

River bank. EDIE *is talking to the old people.*

EDIE: It wasn't even a meeting I needed to go to. There'll be a mediation… if we ever get that far. You don't need to know how it went. Crook. I don't think I'm cut out for this. You might want to find someone else.

1931.

JIM *has returned with a cloth-wrapped bundle. It's covered in dirt.*

JIM: It's been buried. It's yours.

> *He unwraps the parcel, and the layers of newspaper.*

When I was in town they were digging stuff up at the Yumba they'd hidden over the years, to take with them. Remember that night when Abraham got sent away for being on the grog? That night of the fire in your mother's quarters?

ALICE: Eleven years this August. The year Vera died.

> ALICE *unwraps the final layers of the bundle. It's an old journal filled with pieces of paper filed away between the yellowing pages. It is filled with dust and dirt.*

It's Papa's. His Day Book and Journal. His writings from… from the beginning. This is his. We thought it had been burnt.

> *Pause.*

JIM: Everyone feels bad. Still. You got it now. Will you be right? You've got enough water?

Isaac Drandich as Jim in the 2003 HotHouse Theatre production.
(Photo: Jules Boag)

ALICE: Yes…

JIM: Won't be too long.

Present day.

EDIE *is on the riverbank.*

EDIE: Yes indeed. Three days I sat in that office. Right across the road from the supermarket. After that meeting I looked out, on my tod, a very good view of the pastoralists getting their groceries. And not one person made that walk from Safeway's to our door. A town full of questions and there I am sitting up like Jackie. You'd have thought someone would have said, well all right, she got steamed up, but so did everyone, let's go hear her side of things. See what this really means. Three days, no one. Old Sheila said, never mind, love, you're dealing with some of the most ignorant people in the country but… this is the mouth that said 'if any of you had any brains', so I'm not pumping up my own tyres. I thought I could stay calm. You might want to get someone else, I might not have the temperament. I worry about that connection report, I do. Major Mitchell wrote us up all right, and every day we keep adding bits to those family trees, but we'd be foolish not to be worried about those gaps. Aunty Sheila used to go way back and back, but even on a good day now her memory's in and out like a feeding bird, and old Uncle Jim goes on and on about a cave of paintings that he was always told were Yirralong, but he's taken us to the wrong place that many times in the end Lorraine said, 'You've been watching that Discovery Channel. Getting yourself mixed up with some other mob. Like Eskimos.' Now he thinks she's right. Anyway. If you want someone else you can send me a sign.

CATHY *appears. Both women scream.*

Aaaah!

CATHY: Aaaaah!

They recover. CATHY *is carrying a picnic rug and a thermos.*

EDIE: I didn't— I didn't hear a car— I didn't hear you.

CATHY: I parked— sorry— I didn't see you until… I wasn't sure this was the track.

EDIE: That way. And that way. No one usually comes here. Suddenly it's George Street.

CATHY: Nice day.

EDIE: It's where I come to think.

> CATHY *hesitates, which way to go...*

CATHY: Well. Leave you to it.

EDIE: There's a sandy beach sort of thing along that way. Through the scrub. That's the way he went.

CATHY: Who?

EDIE: He didn't expect to see anyone here either. [*Pause.*] Alan the bank manager. He had a towel with him. Tell him he wants to watch the water snakes if he decides to have a swim.

> *Pause.*

CATHY: I'm sorry?

> EDIE *smiles.*

I'm not sure I know what you find so amusing.

EDIE: I'm neutral. I'm just standing here directing traffic.

> CATHY *hesitates, then begins to walk in the opposite direction from the one that* EDIE *indicated.*

Cathy. I'm going to stay here for a while.

CATHY: Good.

EDIE: And a bank manager wouldn't be able to take that long a break.

CATHY: Honestly, Edie, I don't know what you mean.

EDIE: So after all your planning and whatever coded conversations it took yourself to get here, and all the nice little delicacies to nibble in your pack there, you're just going off to sit and eat on your own.

CATHY: Who did you say was along there?

EDIE: Our swashbuckling bank manager. Half your luck.

CATHY: I beg your pardon.

EDIE: Go and meet up with him and discuss your interest rates. If no one knows no one will know. Good luck to you. I'm not going to gossip, I've got a bit more dignity than that. And a bit more on my plate.

> *Pause.*

CATHY: I felt for you at the meeting. The men gave you a bit of a mauling.

EDIE: The men held the floor all right. Made me think I might organise a meeting of our own. Just women. [*Pause.*] Time's ticking. You're just going to have to trust me. As easy and as difficult as that.

As CATHY *heads towards the bank manager...*

By the way, Josslyn my eldest had a postcard from your Tessie. Just the other day. She hasn't spoken to her since netball days. Just her name on it, nothing else. Is she all right?

CATHY: Good. Marvellous. Terrific. Thank you.

1931.

ALICE *is poring over the old journal.* JIM *returns.*

ALICE: At last—I've been willing you to get back.

JIM: How's your scone?

ALICE: The same—better. And reading this is… Jim, listen. I've got a proposition to make.

JIM: A proposition? Dora'll kill me.

ALICE: Very funny.

JIM: I should stick with Dora, thanks all the same.

ALICE: A serious proposition. Reading this journal, Jim—you have to read it—it's like my father talking to me. I was six when he died, and now he's here again. And there's so much and… he was a wonderful man.

JIM: That's true. The Quiet Wise One the old grandfather used to call him.

ALICE: Your grandfather's in here. When my father first set up camp. How the old blacks came to help.

JIM: Other whitefellas'd be looking at their maps, looking for their claims, they'd get pointed off in the wrong direction. 'Hundred miles west', the old blacks'd say. 'Good riddance to bad rubbish, that's the last we'll see of them.' But your father had ears, he could listen. My grandfather always said that.

ALICE: He writes that the Yirralong were landlords, how we were here on your terms. Listen. [*She reads.*] 'Long detours this month on

Ambertrue. Some central parts of the property are closed to whites
for three more weeks, while the Yirralong celebrate their private
ceremonies connected with the moon.'

JIM: I remember them as a kid.

ALICE: The grace my father used to say was black saviours, white
pioneers. And he'd approve of what I'm about to say, I know he
would. [*Pause.*] My proposition is this. I'm going to pass Ambertrue
onto you. In my will. If you want to stay here. If we could keep on
working together. If your family would want to keep working this
land when I'm gone. Under white man's law.

JIM: Now I know you're seeing stars.

ALICE: I've never been more sure of anything in my life. Look what I
found in here [*the journal*]. From 1884. It's a survey he filled in, and
never sent. [*Reading*] 'A survey on the Australian race. E.M. Curr,
Melbourne. Kindly return by August, 1884.'

JIM: It's a bit overdue. Forty-seven years.

ALICE: Eighty-three questions. About tribal life. Father's drawn the
Ambertrue boundary and the tribal boundaries. 'Describe the rules
of marriage in your area.' He's plotted out all the groups—Emu,
Snake, Eagle…

JIM *looks at the journal.*

The survey asks the population levels. Describe any warfare that
occurred during settlement. If native numbers are declining state
the reasons. Father writes down '… bloody warfare, the Native
Police, and my fellow pastoralists poisoning natives like vermin.' He
keeps referring to the 'colonial invasion'. There are clippings from
newspapers here—letters he wrote to the editor saying exactly that.
And from others all over Queensland, graziers who felt uncomfortable
about what was going on. He kept all these for a reason. And you
can guess why he didn't send this survey back.

JIM: Yes. I imagine I can.

ALICE: Protection for the Yirralong. In case it got into the wrong hands.

JIM: That's right.

ALICE: When the show comes up this way there'll be a solicitor. We
can have a new will written up. At the moment, if I die, that cousin
Lonergan takes over this lease.

JIM: Him? The vegetable patch king.

ALICE: Lonergan who comes up every Christmas and goes home with hands cleaner than when he arrived.

JIM: No offence, but he'd worry sheep, that fella. If we had any. Remember that time I let him come out branding, I thought he was going to brand himself. [*Pause.*] I will read that [*the journal*]. I'd like to.

ALICE: What would Dora say, to this idea?

JIM: Dora'd say… let's just bump Alice off right now and get the jewellery as well…

ALICE: I don't have any jewellery.

JIM: Foiled again. [*Pause.*] I don't know.

ALICE: It's a commitment.

JIM: Yep.

ALICE: You, me, Dora, we'll all go in at Show Week. Get it written up properly. And I'll write a letter to Lonergan, so there won't be any challenges, no nasty surprises. All I know is that this [*the journal*] puts us somewhere. My family. And yours. It's our history of our time together. We're part of this. A continuum. It's not my role—or your role—to stop that continuum now.

> *She holds out her hand.* JIM *extends his. Just as they're about to shake on it, her legs give way.*

I really need to get out of the sun.

> JIM *helps her to her feet, and leads her offstage to some shade.*

END OF ACT ONE

ACT TWO

Present day.

LON*'s head appears, followed by* TOM*'s.*

LON: Ssssh. There. There they are. You can just see the top of the tent. Down there on the riverbank.

TOM: They're pig-shooters, Lon. I gave them permission.

LON: I don't have them. When you shift to my place I don't have them. Your brother Paul can have hordes of them here if he wants, but I don't.

TOM: I know that.

LON: They shed. Rubbish, toilet paper, God knows what.

TOM: Mostly they pick up.

LON: They're blow-ins. Couldn't care less. Drive a couple of hundred ks to shoot pigs, no idea of where they are. They can't shut a gate. Black white brindle, electricity or Telstra, they can't shut gates. You wouldn't know now, you wouldn't know what gates they left open last night. What they'll leave open today.

TOM: They're usually all right.

LON: Not to mention these Yirra-wrong wanting to wander round with a cask of moselle under their arm. Let's not mince words, connection to the land, my arse.

TOM: Yirralong.

    Pause.

LON: We can't get lethargic about this. Now we've got Rodney Crittenden on our side, people can get complacent. Sure, Crittenden's good, look what he did with the wharfies. But a leader's only as good as his army. There won't be any bucketloads of extinguishment, unless he knows we're behind him. Turning up to meetings. [*Pause.*] I think of you as a son. I think of you as the son I never had.

Pause.

TOM: I might not be at tomorrow's meeting.

LON: I knew you were going soft on this.

TOM: I'm heading off to Barlow. To your cousin's. To talk to Tessie. Bring her home.

LON: She's fine, hunky dory. Kicking up her heels before the big day.

TOM: She sent me something odd in the mail.

LON: What?

TOM: A shoe.

LON: What do you mean, a shoe?

TOM: A shoe. One of her shoes.

LON: That'd be some sort of artistic statement. She's always making those.

TOM: I'll need your cousin's address.

LON: I need you here. And the truth of the matter is this. No going mentioning it to Cathy.

TOM: What?

LON: She and Tessie have had a row. A tiff. About the wedding, the invitations, who'd know what it was? Tessie's having her little Custer's last stand of independence.

TOM: But not against me.

LON: No but… she just wants to go and visit some relatives, take her time… that sort of thing. Cool down and come home. That'd be what the shoe means. She needs you to be at this meeting.

TOM: Right. And I suppose with this Colin Whelan business… if it's true…

LON: What's that?

TOM: That he's going to put in a second claim. Colin Whelan and his family—mob—whatever they call it. They're going to put in a counter claim. All of what the Yirralong want and more. I thought you would of got told.

LON: Colin Whelan?

TOM: He reckons ATSIC's not too keen on Edie Jordan. Something political like she didn't vote the right way or something.

LON: So…

TOM: So they're saying ATSIC might put some money into Whelan's lawyers. To shove it up the Yirralong lot.

LON: It's Zimbabwe! What they're up to in Zimbabwe! A couple of years time they'll have no whites at all on the land. We could be the last of the line.

    Pause.

TOM: [*noticing, offstage*] The pig-shooters... I better go and see what they want...

LON: Are you going to have Tessie too scared to open her back door? Having her having to step over a mob of half-castes when all she's trying to do is take out the washing. That's why you've got to be at this meeting.

TOM: Right.

LON: Did I ever mention I had some dirt on Edie Jordan?

TOM: No.

LON: It'll cut the hot air straight out of her. I should of used it from the start.

    LON *strides off.* TOM *heads down to the pig-shooters.*

Present day.

The homestead. CATHY *has recently opened a postbag, containing a single, mutilated shoe.*

CATHY: [*talking on the phone*] I'm listening, Tessie, what sort of signs—? Are you sure that's what it meant? I mean just because you see birds flying in an arrow shape doesn't mean that they're pointing somewhere— Where are you Tessie—? I'm not sure that's right— Someone said they saw you down near Barlow. Looking into a river. River bed. Are you near Barlow? It was all we could do to stop Tom jumping in a car to bring you home— Of course no one's following you, of course not. Tom's being very patient, Tessie. But you're going to have to get yourself back here. [*Pause.*] Did something happen, Tessie, that you don't want to come home? Something... I don't know what. [*Pause.*] Well, you know I was thinking of one thing, this is so silly you have to laugh and I do laugh I really do laugh at how silly this is. Apparently there's a rumour going round that I've... I've... I've got a crush on the bank manager. It's so funny. But I thought, gosh, maybe you heard that rumour and maybe you got upset because you thought it was true and you worried your father and I might be having troubles. Which we're not. [*Pause.*] Or maybe you saw me talking to him in town or somewhere else, I might have bumped into him, and thought the worst of me. And got upset— Oh well, that's good. Forget I said all that, silly talk. Because I don't. Have a crush. I don't even know his name. [*Pause.*] We're just trying to wrack our brains as to why you've… you've evaporated from our lives.

LON *enters.*

[*Continuing on the phone*] We got the shoe— The shoe you sent— Oh, come on, Tessie, it's in your size.

LON *picks up the other phone.*

LON: [*talking on the phone*] It's your father here, Tessie, you sent one to Tom as well. Are you calling off the wedding, is that what this is—? No, I'm with you, Tessie. You tell me. I'm listening— Oh yeah, that's really interesting. Yes, I'm with you. Car numberplates have very deep meanings, they hold the wisdom of the ages in those

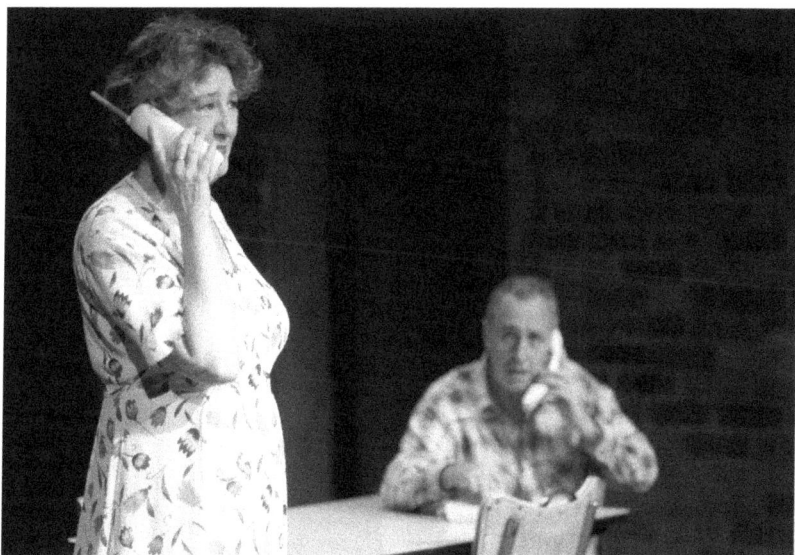

Annie Byron as Cathy and Roger Oakley as Lon in the 2003 HotHouse Theatre production. (Photo: Jules Boag)

three little letters. If we had more passing traffic here I'd probably be running my life by them as well.

CATHY: Sssssh!

LON: [*talking on the phone*] Tessie. Will you do something for your dad? If I ask you to do something, will you do it—? Go and see a doctor, tell him about these signs and see what he's got to say.

The phone goes dead.

How long had she been babbling on like that? Or more to the point how long have you been standing there agreeing with her? The numberplate was E-S-C, so I knew I had to escape. I'm calling the police.

CATHY: You see signs. We all do.

LON: I see signs.

CATHY: You stand on the back verandah, I ask you what are you doing, you tell me you're reading the clouds. Reading the clouds. Seeing what direction the roos are hopping in. Maybe that's what she means.

LON: Do you believe what you're saying?

CATHY: Edie Jordan's eldest girl got a postcard from Tessie just the other day, with nothing on it except her name. What's she trying to say?

LON: Tessie has something wrong with her. [*He picks up the shoe.*] So we have to wake up.

CATHY: If she's frightened of us, she'll never come home. If we can get her home voluntarily, Doctor Rash… Napurti, she'd like him. It's a chemical imbalance, medication they're as right as rain.

LON: We talk to the police. She's up to a week away in any direction of course, unless she got on a train. They can trace her call. They can do that, even to a phone box.

CATHY: She keeps saying she needs her own space. And that she's not missing, if we can speak to her.

LON: Space. What's she got out there? Thousands of square miles she can wander at will. She's mad. Our only child is loony tunes. Congratulations, Tom. Just keep her drugged up and she should remember her name.

CATHY: It's your fault.

LON: Yours is the family with the mad gene.

CATHY: There is no gene. You've cushioned her from this, cushioned her from that. No wonder she hasn't got the internal resources to put her hand up and ask for help. This [*the shoe*] is a cry for something.

LON: When were you talking to Edie Jordan?

CATHY: Sorry?

LON: You were talking to Edie Jordan. When?

CATHY: She phoned.

LON: You went to that women's meeting. You went there behind my back.

CATHY: No I didn't.

LON: Well, you went somewhere, Cathy. If you didn't go to this Edie Jordan gabfest, then where did you go?

CATHY: Nowhere.

LON: The car's done seventy-four ks, Cathy. You went somewhere.

CATHY: Are you checking on me?

LON: I know where you went and I want to hear it out of your mouth.

CATHY: Stop it.

LON: She got you along to this meeting. She got you along to this bullshit ladies' morning tea. 'Native Title and what it means'. Refreshments provided.

CATHY: [*lying*] Yes.

LON: Thank you. Of course I didn't check the bloody speedo. Well, let's hear what you learned then.

CATHY: What?

LON: Come on. You've had the indoctrination. Let's hear what you learned. I'm all ears.

   Pause.

CATHY: You know as well as I do, Lon.

LON: Go on.

CATHY: What they do in other places.

LON: Do tell. You were there.

CATHY: Look, I don't know. It was all in that letter. The abos get permission or something. I don't know.

LON: Would you say, Cathy, that you felt safe in your own home?

CATHY: Yes.

LON: This gets through and you won't. The tyres have been thrown around our necks, and pretty soon we'll be hearing them light the match. And this is not how I want to say goodbye to my country. This is not what I want. You want to talk about books, out there's my book. I'm the chapters. Tom doing it the way I've passed on to him. No one else. [*Pause.*] Sometimes I think you're hoping I'll just drop dead, free you up so you can do what you like. Pal up with Edie Jordan.

CATHY: Don't talk rot.

LON: There are ways to fix Edie Jordan, I should have done this from the start.

He leaves.

1931.

JIM *and* ALICE *have just arrived at a new spot.* JIM *begins collecting ochre.* ALICE *follows him.*

ALICE: Why not?!

JIM: Just the way things are.

ALICE: What way things are? What way?

JIM: You might get hitched.

ALICE: The chap I ordered from the David Jones catalogue doesn't seem to have arrived. And if one ever did, he'd have to abide by my decision. If I outlived you, then it would be left to your boys, and Dora. A solicitor would help us.

JIM: You remember the '24 floods. What do you see when you think of that?

ALICE: People helping each other. Townspeople coming out here to help people off their roofs. The Deltons taking our cattle up to higher ground. Everyone pitching in.

JIM: I saw different.

ALICE: There was nothing different to see. It was a flood, people pitched in. [*Pause.*] What do you mean you saw something different?

JIM: I saw you all helping each other. But to my eye it was *migaloo* helping *migaloo*. And *mardie* helping *migaloo*. But not the other way round. If the Yumba got flooded, not too many *migaloo* rushing out there to help blackfellas. This caper, running cattle, managing a place like this, you're lifting each other up, giving each other advice… and teaching each other this type of feed, that breed of cattle. You're doing that all the time.

ALICE: That's what mother thought when father died. 'Men on the land won't take me seriously', she said. But she earnt her stripes. And they did. And we'd run Ambertrue together.

JIM: They might turn on you. And I'm thinking about my boys. I've been called a uppity nigger often enough, I don't wish that on them.

ALICE: What have you got to lose? What's that saying… the one about stars…?

JIM: I don't know.

ALICE: If you reach for the stars and you fall, you fall on clouds. If you reach for the clouds and fall you hit the ground. Old *migaloo* saying.

JIM: That's a good one. And you know the one thing I can't get out of my head… is the thought of that cousin Lonergan…

A look between them. After a moment he holds out his hand. Now they shake.

Present day.

EDIE *and* LON *have arranged to meet on the riverbank.*

EDIE: If you've got a posse hidden up there, my family's expecting me home to cook tea.

LON: Alone as a new-born babe. [*Pause.*] I haven't been here for years. You still come here to think?

EDIE *glances to the pathway that* CATHY *took in the earlier scene.*

EDIE: There's a bit more pedestrian traffic than there used to be…

Pause.

LON: Round here's the spot I found you that day.

EDIE: Get on with it, Lonergan.

LON: You were a tiny thing and you were sobbing your heart out. Just found out you were pregnant again. With Steve. How is he, by the way? Difficult thing, detox, I'm told. Bounce in and out like a tennis ball on a string.

EDIE: How can I help you, Lon?

LON: First up, no more getting my wife along to your secret womens' meetings. She doesn't want to go again, she doesn't want you bothering her with any more calls.

> *Pause.*

EDIE: [*with irony*] Rightio.

LON: And, as I said on the phone, I think we got off to a bad start that first meeting. It didn't help matters.

EDIE: Oh, I'm used to all sorts of meetings. That's where the word 'Aboriginal' comes from. Attendee of meetings.

LON: You've certainly tossed the grenade in the fish hole all right. For one per cent of the population you don't do a bad job of putting the wind up the rest of us.

EDIE: Two. Two per cent.

LON: People are getting ready to come down on you like a ton of bricks.

EDIE: Having been stirred up by people like you. Who have been stirred up by MPs who get the banks to stir you up some more.

LON: People round here'd hold onto their land if it was slipping off the planet and into outer space.

EDIE: For God's sake, Lon, it's me you're talking to. The only way a pastoralist can lose their bloody land is they break the conditions of their lease. Don't drag yourself down to the same level as that Prime Minister—

LON: Go easy—

EDIE: 'I promise you won't lose your land.' That's as slippery a piece of lying as I've ever heard.

LON: It's a heated debate.

EDIE: Fire's getting plenty of stoking.

> *Pause.*

LON: It all seemed we were getting along not too bad. Your… community. And us. [*Pause.*] And apparently now everyone's in on the act. [*Pause.*] Colin Whelan's tribe. [*Pause.*] Yeah, that worries you and it should. Because they'll have first-class lawyers and you'll be fighting them the same time fighting us. [*Pause.*] I hear they're only doing it because you are. You drop your claim, the whole sorry bunfight could be averted.

EDIE: You seem to hear a lot, Lon. That black grapevine's going overtime.

LON: You could be in court for years.

EDIE: Not with mediation.

LON: Don't kid yourself.

EDIE: Old Aunty Lydia used to say, beware of people who hunt with their mouths. I'm beware.

LON: Just when young Stevie needs you most.

EDIE: He's twenty-three.

Pause.

LON: Think about pulling out. We go back a long way. I don't want to see you get destroyed.

EDIE: Here's what you're afraid of, Lon. An agreement, that we all draw up together. Conditions we decide together. We Yirralong people are recognised as the traditional owners, our responsibilities for visiting these leases, they're all written down.

LON: Is that it?

EDIE: Pretty much.

LON: Well, let's just say that works, which it wouldn't, let's say that works for us because we know each other. I don't know your next generation. I don't know what they'll be like. Your Steve, for instance.

EDIE: Works both ways, Lon. What's your next generation going to be like? Leap of faith. Same as we've made all our lives.

LON: You never knew these rights existed before you got all stirred up.

EDIE: They've always existed. They never went away. We've just been too flaming busy keeping ourselves alive. This isn't an idea that just dropped out of the sky. Go back. Where did your pastoral lease come from?

LON: Lonergan Andrews.

EDIE: Your father. And before that?

LON: [*losing patience*] His cousin Alice. Whose family worked this place up from scratch.

EDIE: The concept? The idea of leases?

LON: They wanted the land opened up.

EDIE: That's it?

LON: Yes, that's it, and it's been back-breaking work.

EDIE: Lord Earl Grey, Lon. In the 1850s—

LON: Shit, we'll be here all day if we go back that far—

EDIE: —knew that blacks couldn't just be shunted off their land, that there had to be a way to co-exist.

LON: Pooncy lace scarf around his neck—Oh, I say, cup of Earl Grey, old chap—

EDIE: He said clearly in legislation, the cattle and the cultivation can't deprive the native of the right to water, the right to hunt—

LON: I don't need a history lesson, thanks—

EDIE: It's *all* you need. Which is why leases had restrictions in them. A moral obligation.

LON: You're not Aborigines anymore… you're something else.

EDIE: Nothing is stronger in my heart, and everyone I represent, than this. We know our rightful country. We've got no choice except to look after it. And sit there, and *be*. And listen to what it has to say and get guidance. We're not well unless we can do that.

LON: You grew up on the Yumba. Go and sit down there, that's still vacant land.

EDIE: Nothing to do with where we grew up—

LON: The spirits, here we go—I'll tell you something, there are days I stand on Ambertrue and I'm part of the air.

EDIE: Yes. Same for me on my country.

LON: No. My boots aren't on the soil, they're of the soil. Like those clouds scudding across that huge, awesome sky, that country scuds through my veins. Pulsing like a bass guitar. And you and your ilk, you shit on that from a great height. You're the only ones who can feel. You're the only ones who can connect.

EDIE: I know that's what you think, but—

LON: I will not have that taken away from me.

EDIE: I can't take that from you and I wouldn't want to. But I won't go to my grave knowing that I let my kids down, and their kids down. Everyone on this earth's entitled to be proud of who they are. You

Pauline Whyman as Edie in the 2003 HotHouse Theatre production.
(Photo: Jules Boag)

know, we used to plead with the old aunties to tell us things, to teach us language, but they couldn't. They taught us as much as they could—all that walks with me every day—but a lot of stories they couldn't tell. Because there are stories that can only be told on country. Because our language is lined up with place, with events that happen there. And the things we want to pass onto our kids now are in those places. On that country. The old aunties, they'd ache, their eyes would fill with tears because they couldn't go there. And they'd pat us on the head and say maybe one day, and they'd try to forget. We never forgot. This is maybe one day.

> *Pause.*

LON: Actually I think this is pretty much the actual spot I found you that day. Twenty-two years ago. Or so. [*Pause.*] It'd only be a couple of years later abortion'd be legal. [*Pause.*] Pregnant again, and you weren't married to Sam then. And he was off working the docks in Brisbane and the last thing he wanted was another kid. Or that's what I believed. Three hundred dollars was a lot to me. I was a kid myself. But I felt for you and it'd get you to Toowoomba and get the job done. Next thing, to my amazement I see you walking up the main street, up the duff well and truly. The money and the box, not bad going.

EDIE: You've forgotten.

LON: I certainly have not—

EDIE: Yes you have, your history really is fuzzy. Why you ended up giving me that money. Why would you get an Aboriginal woman out of trouble? We used to see each other at rodeos or the pictures once in a blue moon. Why would you have done that?

LON: I'm asking myself that.

EDIE: This is a shameful thing for me to say, Lon, but I'll say it if it'll make you remember. I said to you how different you were from your father. And you asked me what I meant. So I told you how Lonergan senior, your father, how he'd come into town one night, on the drink, when he was still a single man, gone out the Yumba when our men were all out droving, and how he'd got Sheila pregnant. And how she'd used herbs and then some knitting needles and done herself some damage. But got rid of it all the same. You blushed easily when you were younger and your cheeks all fired up.

You knew I was telling the truth and you felt shame. And you said, don't go down that path. I'll give you the money. That's right. When I decided not to go Toowoomba, I gave that money to Sheila. To buy something for herself, pay the rent, whatever she wanted. From the family of the child she never had. I thought that seemed fair all round.

Pause.

LON: So how's your Steve going?

EDIE: I told you.

LON: He mightn't be going so good if he knew all this though, would he? That if you'd had the get up and go to get on a bus, he'd be a memory, if that.

EDIE: Christ, Lon, you wouldn't.

LON: A boy like Steve, that could tip him off the edge.

EDIE: Why would you dream of telling him that?

LON: Because I don't have a lot of time. I'm not a well man. You do what you have to do to tidy up loose ends.

EDIE: How could you even dream of telling him that…?

Pause.

LON: You could go a very different path. You could say to your mob, look. This is just going to be too hard. There's the Telstra land, and the bits of Crown Land. We could just go for that. All those old ladies, they're eating out of your hands. They'll go with what you say. And we could get on with our lives. And everyone'd think, well, she's come to her senses.

EDIE *again looks along the path, to where* CATHY *had her assignation.*

EDIE: So. You could turn my life around like that. In a breath my life might change. But you know something, Lon? I could do the same to you.

LON: You have!

Pause.

EDIE: And you will not communicate with my son. I'll take out an AVO.

LON: Drop the claim and I won't have to. I did not steal that land.

EDIE: Well, someone did and you reap the benefits.

LON: Well, didn't we just have all the luck? That's the way the penny falls.

EDIE: Do anything to me, Lon. Anything you like, but don't go near my son. Your Tessie's not a well girl either. The least you can do is leave our kids out of it.

LON: Tessie's fine.

EDIE: She came to see me before she went away.

LON: What for?

EDIE: I couldn't quite understand her train of thought but it was something about having carved her name somewhere. When she was a kid. She said she was getting more and more worried that she'd been sung. Her words. Not mine.

LON: Been 'sung'?

EDIE: That was the only bit I could understand. It was very clear to me that she's not a well girl either. So the least you can do is understand.

LON: My wife said one of your girls got a postcard. I'd like to have it, please.

EDIE: It's just a postcard.

LON: What of? Where from?

EDIE: Of rock paintings, as a matter of fact. Beautiful, pristine rock paintings. From one of the gorges, somewhere. And just her name on the back.

1931.

ALICE *has found a part of the journal with very fragile, yellowed fold-out paper. Together she and* JIM *are folding it out.*

ALICE: Hold it up… look at this… careful. It's…

> *Slowly they handle the paper, bearing the faint pencil marks of an old family tree.*

We should look at this at home.

JIM: Like a bible…

ALICE: Like a family tree in a bible… but it's your family. How everyone was connected. Look—look how many were Yirralong. There, there, all there.

JIM: Before outsider mobs started coming in.

ALICE: Add this to the one I've sketched out for my book and… this really fills in the gaps. We should fold it back. If the wind catches this…

They fold the page back carefully.

So, whatever we do now, whatever decisions we have to make— finances, buying machinery—equal.

JIM: I wasn't gunna go that far, letting you make decisions.

ALICE smiles, then looks up, slightly off-balance. Her eyesight is troubling her but she's not letting on.

ALICE: Willy wagtail.

JIM: Message bird.

ALICE: That's a message from Father that we're doing the right thing. You know what I'm going to do? Write you a letter of agreement. Just so you know I'm fair dinkum. That it wasn't the bump on the head.

She opens her notebook and eventually makes a few marks on the page. JIM *walks over a rocky outcrop.*

JIM: No, it's not, I thought it was… old blackfella well. But it's not. That one over the south-west boundary has to be ten feet deep. No shovels in them days. We should ride over some time have a look if it's still there.

ALICE: Aren't the colours bright? It's a very… very vivid light. What were we talking about…? Sorry. The things that go… what's the word…?

JIM: In language, Miss Alice? This ground.

ALICE: No, the… the… the hole there. What you were talking about.

JIM: Wells?

ALICE: Wells. Wells. Yes. I'm feeling very parched. I need to…

JIM: Come on…

ALICE: Isn't it just… absurdly bright…?

Present day.

The homestead. LON *is hauling on a heavy hessian bundle, tied 'kerchief' style. He carries a flogging hammer.*

CATHY: What are you doing with those…?

LON: This is not the sort of stuff you have hanging around—out of my way—I'll deal with it. I'm going to deal with it.

CATHY: What are you—what are you doing, Lon?

LON: Stopping people from taking away who I am. Figuring out a way to stand in front of my father's grave and hold my head up high. I think she said something. Edie Jordan. I think Tessie's said something to her. About the rock paintings. Don't look at me like that.

TOM: [*offstage, calling*] Hello? Hello?

LON: Shit.

CATHY: [*calling*] In here, Tom.

> TOM *enters, anxious to show them the map that he's holding.*

TOM: Jack Farley got hold of the map that's gone in with this claim business, asked me to pass it [*the map*] on. Ambertrue's definitely not on it. These little triangles are sacred sights. These squares are the burial grounds. These ones mark the camps. And the waterholes. You're not here. I mean, we're not here. And my place neither.

LON: Doesn't mean we're off the hook.

TOM: But it means we can ease up a bit and concentrate on Tessie. Wherever she is, I'm going to get her. Bring her home. [*To* CATHY] I'm sorry you've had the tiff or whatever… but I'm going down to Barlow whether she likes it or not.

CATHY: She's not there.

TOM: Where is she?

CATHY: Her other cousins. In Charleville.

TOM: Well, ring them right now, tell them to keep her there.

CATHY: The thing is though… they've just had a baby. They often keep the phone turned right down. I'll go and get the number.

LON: [*reading the map*] Bloody Donnigan and his *bora* bloody ring. The tourist attraction. It doesn't matter a fig that we're not here. Doesn't get us off the claim. We've still got to go through the same shit as everyone else. And the courts take this seriously—drawn up from the spirits.

TOM: The old people. And the anthropologist. To be fair.

LON: Old Granny Anderson wouldn't have known her arse from a bullock's foot, never mind where all this was.

TOM: In the long run they'll be more interested in all up here near Taylor's and Moonee Downs… and this burial site over by Possession Creek. So let's just concentrate on getting Tessie back.

LON: [*reading the map*] This is my point. This burial site here is exactly my point! Old Jack's kept tight about that burial site for as long as I can remember. Never mind his best intentions, he's ended up on here.

TOM: Nothing we can do about it now.

> LON *unwraps the hessian bundle.*

LON: None of this exists.

> *It is filled with stone Aboriginal artefacts.*

TOM: Christ.

LON: Some of the old buck niggers gave these to my father, before they went off to Palm Island or whatever resort it was. They could spot an axe-head from that far off. There was some handmade fishing net in here somewhere. They get a search warrant… they find this, suddenly we're on their beaten track.

> TOM *picks up one of the artefacts.*

That one was down near the river, near a bit of old skull. This I broke open to see if it was hollow…

TOM: It's solid.

LON: That's right. Now, are you going to turn these to dust for me, or do I have to do it? Soon as it's done we're in the car to Charleville, go and bring Tessie home.

TOM: Maybe if you called a museum.

> *Pause.*

LON: I'm disappointed in you, Tom. I thought you had the guts.

> LON *starts walloping the hammer. Eventually, as he grows breathless,* TOM *takes the hammer from him… and takes over, taking his frustration and anger out on the stones.*

1931.

JIM, *concerned for* ALICE, *picks up their saddle bags, the journal and her notes.* ALICE *is struggling hard to keep her balance, fighting her panic.*

ALICE: Help please, Jim—

He's trying to help her to her feet.

Jim, do you know I can't actually see? I can see shapes but… Oh, goodness.

JIM: All right. Watch yourself here… careful…

ALICE: It'll just be temporary thing… surely it will…

JIM: We'll need to get you back, get on the radio, get some help…

ALICE: If I sit for a while…

JIM: There's some shade over there… we'll get you in the shade.

ALICE: You've got the journal… and my notes…

JIM: All here, all safe… you'll be right…

ALICE: Is it very far, to the shade…?

JIM: No. You're right…

Present day.

TOM *is smashing the artefacts to pieces. And he's not making much headway.*

LON: Stop.

TOM: Maybe just send them to the museum, in Brisbane. Anonymous.

CATHY *enters. The phone in her hand.*

How'd you go?

CATHY: It's unbelievable. She left an hour ago. If that. If that, they said. If that.

TOM: Let me speak to them. Press redial, let me speak to them. [*Pause. To* LON] We can chuck these into a creek. On the way. To Charleville. We could just leave right now. [*Pause.*] Or… you could tell me what's going on. Put me out of my misery. Tell me what's going on.

Pause.

LON: We don't know.

TOM: Bullshit.

LON: Tessie's not well. That's it. She needs to come home, you're right. We thought it would pass. There are no cousins in Barlow. Or Charleville. She gets… stressed or something. Loses her way.

TOM: So, what, I'm some sort of callous bastard who's going to run a mile because his fiancee's got a few problems?

CATHY: No, no—

TOM: The times she has called I could hear she wasn't herself. And there I was thinking it was me. Or us. If she's having problems I'll get her help. But the first thing is to get her home.

LON: Let's you and I go to Toowoomba. With her photo. That'd be the smart thing to do. Start from there. Start with the dressmaker. Can't be that many there.

CATHY: I'm going to give you the new photo, the one with her longer hair...

CATHY *exits.*

LON: Day after tomorrow we can go, how's that?

TOM: Why not now?

LON: There's something else. Bigger than those things.

TOM: What?

LON: Now you're family you can know. [*Pause.*] That odd bit of rock formation where I border with Ewandale. Where the land drops off to that gully. Where the old man had that stampede of wild cattle that time. There's a cave there. A shelter sort of thing. Covered in flaming paintings.

TOM: Paintings.

LON: On rocks, with the stencils. On rock walls. All over.

TOM: Fair dinkum.

LON: It's not on this map. No one knows about it. Only family. We're the only ones know. Unless someone wandered up there one time that I don't know about. That's the danger. Some bloody long-lost cousin of a town half-caste with enough brain cells left to remember going there once. I don't know if anyone has but that's the possibility. That's the weak spot. [*Pause.*] Painting over won't work, they've got x-rays see through paint. And a claim'd go on it for sure.

TOM: A site of significance.

LON: Don't get me wrong, it's a beautiful spot. I love going up there. But it has to go. The overhang. It's not a small job. It'd take us both. And be between us both. One thing Tessie's going to need when she comes back is stability. No Native Title lawyers wandering over the place. Everything just rolling along nice and calm. That'll be what she needs. [*Pause.*] We could take all these up with us. Do it all in one go. More bang for your buck. Then when Tessie's home... it's all done.

1931.

ALICE *is sitting, supported by* JIM. *She's gulping down water.*

JIM: How's that...?

ALICE: Thank you. I just had an overwhelming thirst, as if I was... parched inside. Every part of me, parched. My eyes are fine now, truly.

JIM: We're going to have to get you back.

ALICE: Just spell a little bit more.

JIM: I'll double you. Come on.

ALICE: I'd just like to have a kip. Just twenty minutes, something like that. Would you mind?

JIM: I don't feel good, letting you have a kip. There's no moon tonight, we'll need to get back.

   Suddenly ALICE *scrambles for her notebook and pen.*

What are you after?

ALICE: I didn't finish... I want to write down our agreement, just so that it's... then I'll have a kip. Leave me.

JIM: I'll go get some more water.

   ALICE *starts to write, but it's clear even to us that she's actually scrawling, scribbling.*

Present day.

The homestead. LON *and* TOM *cross the space, carrying swags and camping equipment and the artefacts in the bundles.* CATHY *follows.*

CATHY: Tom. You're not going to Toowoomba. Tell me where you're going.

LON: To fix some fencing up near the north-west side. To fix some fencing overnight, then Toowoomba tomorrow.

CATHY: Tom?

TOM: Like Lon said. Some fencing's down. It's an overnight job.

CATHY: You're not a very good liar, Tom.

TOM: Well, no offence meant, Cathy, but you are. Whatever's up with Tessie I should have known. We're meant to be getting married. I'm not some stud bull has to be kept in the dark until he's needed. I'm a part of all this.

CATHY: A stud bull? I don't know I've ever thought of you as that…

TOM: It's not a joke. And I'm not a joke. You know what I mean.

> *Pause.*

CATHY: [*to* LON] Where are you going?

LON: Tom I trust with this. You I don't.

> *Pause.*

CATHY: [*calling, to* TOM] You should find out how long he's had that gelignite sitting in that shed.

LON: We'll be back first thing. If you go out, leave that photo on the table.

CATHY: Where would I go out?

LON: You might go out tonight. You'll be free as a bird.

CATHY: Well, I'll just have a great big party, all the middle-aged bachelors and spinsters, round 'em all up.

LON: Just don't go driving at dusk. Or dawn. There's a lot of roos around at the present moment.

CATHY: Why would I go driving?

LON: Cathy, Cathy, Cathy. You're as close to a pane of glass as anyone I've ever known. I know you inside out.

CATHY: No, you don't. You think you know me. No—you think you possess me. Me and Tessie, both of us, that's what you think. You claim us as yours. But that's not the same, Lon. As knowing.

> LON *leaves.* TOM *follows.*

> *Dusk. Outside the cultural co-op office in town.* EDIE *is locking up for the day.* CATHY *is out on the 'street'. She has a large photograph in her hand.*

I… er… I… don't suppose you've seen the sergeant? I'm trying to slip this under the door but… I'm not normally in town this late… everything looks strange all shut.

EDIE: Well, they're still working at the bank. You can see the light on from here.

Pause.

CATHY: I'm only going to ask you this once. Did you say something to my husband?

EDIE: No. Which is not to say I wasn't tempted. I can give that to the coppers tomorrow if you like.

Pause.

CATHY: Lon gave them an old photo of her, God knows why he did that. Before she grew her hair. This is only a year ago, the other one wasn't her. It was old. God knows how long. This is a studio shot, of course, I don't know if they can make her smaller. That's the only thing. Scan it in. And make it smaller. To send to other stations. I'm not sure they can do that. Make her smaller. [*She starts to cry.*] Sorry.

EDIE: Come inside.

They step 'inside'. Throughout this scene the wall of family trees (actual or abstract) gradually becomes more distinct.

CATHY: [*fighting back tears*] Isn't this silly, just the thought of anyone having to be smaller? God. I must be going mad. I don't even know what I mean by that.

Pause. EDIE *passes her a tissue.*

Thank you. [*She takes in the 'family trees'.*] What are these?

EDIE: These are what you're so afraid of. The family trees. Who's related to who.

Pause.

CATHY: What did you mean you were tempted?

EDIE: Mother's instinct. Your husband threatened to hurt my son.

CATHY *makes a noise of disbelief.*

He's a bit like your Tessie, my boy. On the edge.

CATHY: The last thing Lon would do is want to hurt your son. I'm sorry, you misunderstood.

EDIE: You can tell Lon not to waste his breath, the job's been done.

CATHY: What do you mean?

EDIE: He plans to tell my Steve that I'd wanted to get rid of him, that I'd wanted to have an abortion. It's true. I did. Until I saw him born.

CATHY: Why would Lon do that?

EDIE: So I'd convince people to withdraw our claim. And because he knows my Steve's on the edge. Every time I leave that house my heart sits in my throat and I hope to God I've cleared the hoses, or the ropes or the ammunition. You can tell Lon I got to him before he did. I told Steve the story. Told him I love him. What he does with it's up to him.

CATHY: Lon gets... het up.

EDIE: You want me to give the sergeant the photograph tomorrow? You can just leave it here.

CATHY *hesitates.*

I say I'll do something, I'll do it.

CATHY *puts down the photo and runs her finger across the family trees.*

CATHY: All those question marks...

EDIE: You know the first thing she taught us, my mother? Same as her mother taught her. First thing a black woman teaches her kids... is how to do without you. First thing they've got to learn. How to survive if they're taken away. My kids learnt that from when they were babies. That's what the question marks are about. You'd leave taking your kids to doctors until you really had to, worried they'd call it neglect.

CATHY: It was a terrible business, all that.

EDIE: My daughter manages a company, travels all over the world, still she's got that at the back of her mind. And now you've got a question mark. Your girl. Happens to us all, black, white or indifferent. Never taught mothers how to do without their kids.

CATHY: My daughter will come home.

EDIE: That's what our people thought.

CATHY: It's not the same.

EDIE: My missing child's more missing than yours? I suppose if that gets you through the night.

CATHY *tries to answer, but can't. Fighting tears, she goes.*

1931 and the present.

ALICE *is sitting, eyes down in her notebook, pen in hand.* JIM *is pouring some water into a cup.*

JIM: How you feeling now?

ALICE: Good! It is marvellous! All of it.

JIM: This won't happen again. If the first ride hadn't been so fast, Ginger wouldn't have baulked you. Your first ride in months… I got to learn to control my temper, you're right.

> *Suddenly* ALICE *slumps forward. He grabs her, feels her pulse, and begins to shake her.*

Alice. Oh, Jesus. No. No! No!

> *The sound of an enormous explosion. Rocks cracking.* LON *runs on.*

LON: Oh, Jesus… Jesus… Tom! Here! Tom!

JIM: Miss Alice. Please.

> TOM *enters. He's grabbed a towel to cover his bleeding hand.* JIM *is shaking* ALICE, *trying to revive her. He slaps her.* ALICE*'s notebook has fallen out of her hands and onto the ground.* JIM *carefully places* ALICE *down, and picks it up.*

LON: [*to* TOM] We're right… you're right… Jesus. Fuck, the blood. We'll get you in the truck.

JIM: [*to* ALICE] I won't leave you. I won't.

TOM: I think my hand's gone.

> JIM *looks at the final pages and turns it upside down. This doesn't make it any clearer. He hesitates. He almost decides to take the book, but then carefully puts it into her bag, closing it tight, and placing it next to her.*

LON: Fuck. Oh, fuck.

JIM: I'll sit with you a while…

LON: Elevated… keep it… elevated.

LON *runs off in a panic.* JIM *takes in the landscape.*

JIM: We had a dream. For half a day…

LON *re-enters.*

LON: Come on. Anyone asks, we were blowing rocks for a dam. Blowing rocks for a dam. Fuck, Jesus. The blood. You don't worry. I'll be right to drive.

They exit as… CATHY *appears in a slip. Silence except for the sound of cockatoos.*

CATHY: I know… I know… I know… I know… I do know… I do know… [*Calling*] I know you! I know you, Tessie, I know you won't come back. And I know this place, I know. We'll disappear in the topsoil. All of us in a willy willy, swirled up in the debris and the dust. Scattered. Gone.

JIM: We had a dream for half a day… and that's the end of that.

JIM *lifts* ALICE *and carries her off.*

Transition.

Time has passed. A street. CATHY, *with a cardboard box, is moving house.* EDIE, *with a plate of sandwiches, is carrying her car keys.*

CATHY: Oh. Hello.

EDIE: Cathy.

CATHY: Moving day. We're moving. We've moved. Into the townhouses up that drive. Here in town. A change.

EDIE: Lon's heart not too good, I hear.

CATHY: You can't keep having heart attacks and… Yes… nice and close to the clinic.

EDIE *nods to the sandwiches.*

EDIE: One of our old aunties finally passed over.

CATHY: Yes, I saw the funeral…

EDIE: Her family lives over there. The red brick house with the bright blue door. You'll be neighbours.

CATHY: Oh…

CATHY *looks across to the house. Behind them,* TOM *wheels* LON *out to supervise proceedings from a distance. He wears an oxygen mask.* TOM*'s arm is heavily bandaged, so he wheels* LON *with one hand.*

EDIE: I'm first here… There'll be a big wake. Reminds me of Old Granny Anderson—

CATHY: Here's Tom come to give me a hand. Oh. Sorry.

TOM: Edie.

EDIE: How's your arm, Tom?

TOM: Be a bit better with something on the end.

EDIE: I was just thinking about old Granny Anderson. You remember her?

TOM: I remember her. I do.

EDIE: She said she wasn't waiting to die to have a wake. She had hers about two years before she passed over. Made us all get up there under the bough shed on the Yumba and tell her what we were going to say about her. She enjoyed it, too.

    Pause.

TOM: I never talked to her. We were always told to steer clear.

EDIE: She was lethal, Granny Anderson. You shoulda steered clear. If your father was still alive, he'd tell you.

TOM: She was always onto council about something, I remember he used to say that.

EDIE: She'd get ropeable. After the war when the RSL built the pool… there was a lot of discussion. Should Aboriginal children be allowed in? The council said no. Black skin might flake off, wreck the filter, who knows? And Granny Anderson heard about this and up she goes to council. And got all those men in one room. 'Aboriginal soldiers fought in that war. All right, Aboriginal kids can't go in the pool, that's your decision. All right. But I just wanted to let all you men know that I'll be taking a chair down there outside that lovely white wall you've built. And every white kid goes in through those turnstiles, I'll let them know the names of their black 'lations. Uncles, aunts, half-brothers and sisters. The lot.' Two days later a unanimous vote. By the end of the week the pool was filled with little black kids doing bombs in the deep end. A good twenty years before Moree.

Pause.

TOM: I'm related. Aren't I? To Granny Anderson.

CATHY: Tom's on medication.

EDIE: Yes you are, Tom. You sure are.

TOM: Her father was my great-grandfather, right? Right?

EDIE: Yes.

TOM: I heard once, but I was never sure. They just used to say we had Greek blood in us.

CATHY: I don't think you're on the family tree they've…

EDIE: She was a good old stick.

TOM: Well. That's food for thought. Excuse me.

He goes back up to LON.

CATHY: He keeps hoping Tessie might have turned up. But she hasn't. She rang. I told her about Lon. But all she could talk about was how she was tip-toeing along the edges of canyons. She sounded 'up' but she'll plummet again and…

EDIE: You don't know where she is.

CATHY: She won't say. He keeps hoping she'll just turn up. She probably will. We've told her that we've moved. [*Pause.*] While Lon was in hospital, Edie, I went over to the bank.

EDIE: You don't muck around. Shit. Sorry. I've got a quick tongue. That was… I'm sorry. Uncalled for. Good luck to you whatever happens.

CATHY: I'm going to give you something, don't open it, don't let Lon see that I'm giving it to you. Is he watching?

EDIE: Tom's wheeling him inside.

CATHY *gets the journal and Alice's notebook, both still wrapped in the old cloths.*

CATHY: I don't know what you need for that connection report, or if it helps with all those question marks, but this might have something in it.

EDIE *slowly unwraps the larger book.*

I read them once, years ago. I think you might be able to use them. They've been in the safety deposit box for years. Lon's the only one with the key, but it always helps to know the bank manager, as they say. A journal and day book, then the old aunty's jottings and memories. It's not a novel. That was something Lon said. That it was all a novel. But it's not. You could photocopy it. And give it back. It looks hard to read but… once you get used to it, it becomes easier. Once you get used to the scrawls and flourishes. There are lots of names, and a family tree, at least that's what it looks like. It might fill in the gaps.

EDIE *opens it and begins to read.* CATHY *watches her.*

Music.

THE END